50 YEARS OF THE

THOROUGHBRED CLUB

POWER AND PASSION OF RACING PALS

ROD NICHOLSON

WP

Published by:
Wilkinson Publishing Pty Ltd
ACN 006 042 173
Level 4, 2 Collins St Melbourne, Victoria, Australia 3000
Ph: +61 3 9654 5446
www.wilkinsonpublishing.com.au

NATIONAL LIBRARY OF AUSTRALIA

A catalogue record for this book is available from the National Library of Australia

Thoroughbred Club — Power and Passion of Racing Pals
Planned date of publication: 09-2018
Title: Thoroughbred Club — Power and Passion of Racing Pals
ISBN(s): 978-1-925642-63-6: Printed — Hardcover

Front cover: Rekindling ridden by Corey Brown wins the 2017 Melbourne Cup at Flemington in Melbourne, Victoria. (Photo by Michael Klein / Newspix)
Back cover: Owners, Kevin Bamford and Gerry Ryan, pose with the trophy after their racehorse, Americain, ridden by jockey Gerald Mosse won the 2010 Melbourne Cup at Flemington. (Photo by Michael Dodge / Newspix)
Colour section images: Rod Nicholson, Colin Bull and Anthony McKee.

Design: Michael Bannenberg
Printed in China.

INTRODUCTION

A MEANDER through the throng at any Thoroughbred Club luncheon is a history lesson. As members chat they recount tales of the turf, exchange betting plunge stories, recall historic races and champion racehorses (and usually add the "hacks" they owned and raced themselves). They are serious about racing's image, its issues and challenges, and moments later are laughing as a member recounts a funny yarn, usually involving the punt and too much amber fluid.

The people who make up this club have a unique insight into racing. Many are breeders, owners, bookmakers, administrators, stewards or trainers and jockeys. They are intricately involved and informed privately or at Thoroughbred Club functions by the people who walk the corridors of power within the industry, as well as government. The members, who come from all walks of life, are passionate about racing. For many it is their livelihood, for others it is a way of life that offers the chance to mingle with friends and enjoy the sport of kings.

The passion and the influence within the club is palpable. Anyone who has attended a Caulfield Cup eve or Blue Diamond Stakes eve luncheon will testify to the club's enthusiasm for racing. That it attracts elite guest speakers from the training, riding, administrative and media ranks, as well as world-class entertainers, is confirmation of its "pull" within the racing ranks.

The year 2018 marks the 50th anniversary of the Thoroughbred Club and this book is designed not only to record its history, but importantly to bring to life many of the characters who have built and now oversee the club.

A flick through the pages reveals the diversity of the clan. They range from builders, car salesmen, breeders, racing administrators, real estate agents, pharmacists, insurance agents, the media and even priests!

What all have in common is a love of the thoroughbred, and the chance to have fun with a group of equally enthusiastic racing folk.

This book reflects that and is a combination of considerable efforts by many members, notably former secretary Ian Scroggie and current secretary Roger Jennings. The club also would like to thank the sponsors whose generosity contributed to the production of this book — club members Peter

Devitt (L.U. Simon Builders Pty Ltd), Cameron Fisher (Changing Places Real Estate), Jared Lechte (Mercedes-Benz Mornington), Neville Gibson (Honan Insurance Group) and Roger Jennings (Betta Stone).

To those who gave so freely of their time to recount their involvement in the Thoroughbred Club and racing, thank you. I hope your power and passion is duly reflected in these pages.

ROD NICHOLSON

FOREWORD

Thoroughbred Club President, Cameron Fisher

THE Thoroughbred Club encapsulates the essence of the racing industry, uniting administrators, owners, breeders, trainers, jockeys and punters in the common love of racing and the horse.

The year 2018 celebrates 50 years since the establishment of the Thoroughbred Club, which has evolved into one of the most influential and respected promoters of racing in the nation.

Along the journey the club has been guided by inspirational leaders, most notably Henry Harrison who was president for 25 of the first 50 years. And for all but six months of the first half-century only three secretaries — David and Ian Scroggie and Roger Jennings — guided the club. The latter two were instrumental in recounting much of the history revealed in this book.

Club members have come from all walks of life, as have their guests at functions, highlighted every year by the Caulfield Cup eve luncheon that in the modern era has attracted more than 800 avid racing fans.

The club also can boast an exceptional list of guest speakers who have entertained, educated, provoked or promoted racing. The ilk of Captain Mark Phillips, Ron Walker and Sir Zelman Cowan, innumerable top administrators, comedians including Sir Les Patterson (Barry Humphries), media personalities and sporting stars have shared a wealth of knowledge and life experiences.

From the Hotel Australia to the Southern Cross and Leonda to the Caulfield racecourse, the club has moved with the times, growing from a maximum of 20 members a half century ago, 55 in 1982, 108 in 2001 to today's membership list of 186. Besides mingling to talk horses and racing, the club also has indulged in a prime objective: fun.

From Christmas parties with Santa arriving in a helicopter to dinner dances to days on club member Geoff Robertson's yacht to golf tournaments to visits to stud farms, club members have enjoyed fun activities over the years.

To cap off 50 years, former club president John Connellan organised a gala black-tie evening at Rippon Lea which, with mind-boggling accessories (read a scantily-clad hostess in a giant champagne glass and similar delights), was likened to a Hollywood bash.

The club has been instrumental in promoting racing. In fact, it has boasted its own race for the past 50 years, growing the Thoroughbred Club Stakes into a Group 3 feature.

And club members have been associated with champions, including Taj Rossi, Manikato and Sobar, as well as Melbourne and Caulfield Cup winners.

While honouring the past, the club always looks to the future. The establishment in 2016 of the Colts, limited to 20 members under the age of 40, was designed to entice younger members into the fold to carry on the legacy of 50 years of dedicated promotion of racing.

HENRY HARRISON was the president of the Thoroughbred Club for 25 of its first 50 years, and a dominant figure at the club from late 1971 until his death in September of 2005, aged 91.

He was a Life Member (1985) and after his presidency between 1974 and 1999 he became the club's Patron in Chief. They are the mere statistics which cannot record the impact Harrison had on the club.

As long-time secretary Ian Scroggie points out, Harrison ruled the club with an iron fist. His most famous saying, recounted by countless members, was repeated virtually annually during his presidency.

"I would like any nomination for president in the same envelope as your letter of resignation"

"Nominations for president and the committee are coming up and I welcome your nomination. I would like any nomination for president in the same envelope as your letter of resignation."

Geoff Dawson, who also became club president, said his father-in-law Harrison "put the club on the map."

"We joined at the same time (November of 1971) and he had taken over within three years and fashioned the club into a major influence on the racing scene. He set it up for the leaders who followed, establishing the foundation and showing everyone the way with his drive, enthusiasm and entrepreneurial skills," he said.

"Henry was a very fair and genuine person. He loved his family; he was a real honourable man," Dawson said.

Another former president, Gary Lechte, also hailed Harrison's achievements.

"To say he was ahead of his time is a gross understatement. Henry was always most influential and was able to initiate this influence on both sides of politics, for the good of racing."

He also marvelled at his unquenchable optimism.

“On a visit to hospital (not long before Harrison’s death in September of 2005) with Henry’s horse trainer Bevan Laming, I had trouble finding his ward, until that is, I heard my name being enthusiastically called out from the end of the hall some 20 metres away.

“Always the optimist was Henry. He wanted to talk about his yearlings and their potential. Bevan commented to me later that at 91 years of age you would think you would be more concerned with your older horses. Not Henry Harrison.” Harrison, who owned a thriving business in Richmond manufacturing toolboxes for tradesmen, was a “Mr Fixit” whose strength was dealing with politicians and businessmen.

And he had friends in high places, particularly the state’s sport ministers of the time — Brian Dixon, Neil Trezise and Tom Reynolds. As an example of his “means to an end” he introduced long-serving Liberal premier Sir Henry Bolte to greyhound racing, giving him smart performer Bold Brat in 1971.

Yet he was the same man who loved standing on the terraces at the Port Melbourne Football Ground supporting his beloved “Borough” with the Painters and Dockers. Harrison owned many gallopers — he was particularly keen on the evergreen Donnie Brasco which he raced with club members Lechte, Dawson and Martin Godby — as well as All Shot, who won two William Reid Stakes, in 1973 and ’74, and was runner-up in another.

However most in the racing industry will recall Harrison for his contribution to greyhound racing, in which he was involved for 60 years.

His notable achievements involved 28 years on the Sandown GRC committee (1959-1987), including 23 of them as chairman from 1964. He also served two years on the Greyhound Racing Control Board and had the honour of being the first president of the Australian Greyhound Racing Association in 1963.

His greyhound racing passion dated back to the 1920s, initially as a typical punter and owner-breeder. He witnessed his first Melbourne Cup, in the proprietary days of the sport, at Napier Park in 1927. And when the race shifted to Sandown Park in 1956, with the introduction of the tin hare, Harrison was a powerful force in developing its status.

Harrison’s greatest achievement, according to Dawson who followed him as SGRC president, was the negotiation of TAB coverage for greyhound racing through his powerful connections in the racing industry and with high ranking state politicians. "He was extremely convincing, and I don't think the SGRC would be here today without his influence," Dawson said. "He even purchased a thoroughbred from Sir Chester Manifold, just to speak to him about his main objective: getting the tote for the greyhounds."

From the mid-1960s to late-1980s, Harrison was the sport's visionary. The patriarch of Sandown Park was an administrative chameleon — autocratic and a people's man. He was pro-Sandown GRC, much to the chagrin of the National Coursing Association of Victoria.

Harrison displayed political nous securing off-course TAB coverage on metropolitan greyhound racing in 1966 — a watershed in the sport's history. He was also at the SGRC helm during the introduction of computerised totalisator equipment in 1974, which generated exponential growth in on-course betting.

Harrison was co-founder of the Commonwealth Greyhound Racing Association in the early 1960s — now the Australian Greyhound Racing Association, of which he was the first president. He served for a short period as a Greyhound Racing Control Board member, where he was instrumental in many government changes to the sport. Harrison also received a Centenary Medal for service to greyhound racing in Victoria.

Harrison also demonstrated entrepreneurial skill and promotional flair in delivering a huge profile to the Melbourne Cup (of greyhounds).

"He was instrumental in bringing out film stars and sporting celebrities for the Melbourne Cup — including Christopher George, Robert Stack, Elke Sommer, and even Greg Norman," Dawson said. "The movie stars would come back to my farm on the weekend for a 'Melbourne Cup after-party'. It was also a family reunion/picnic day, a real social event with around 250 people."

Plans to build the new grandstand at Sandown Park were conceived in 1982 and came to fruition in 1986 with the $4m construction of a predominantly glass structure, the design of which substantially influenced the architecture of the current Caulfield racecourse grandstand. The Henry Harrison Grandstand is testimony to the club's father figure's enormous contribution to the SGRC and the greyhound industry in general. For all that, he always will be remembered as the backbone of the Thoroughbred Club.

THOROUGHBRED CLUB

LIFE MEMBERS

H A Hall	1970
W C Cayley	1980
J H (Bunny) Thomson	1982
H Harrison	1985
S E Leighton	1990
H A Evans	1992
K Heffernan	1992
G A Bellmaine	1996
J M Russell	2001
I D Scroggie	2004
G T Dawson	2006
J Dillon	2008
M Kostos	2013
G Lechte	2015
F Bayne	2018

PRESIDENTS

Hal A Hall	1968-1970
Warrick C Cayley	1970-1974
Henry Harrison	1974-1999
John Dillon	1999-2001
Geoff T Dawson	2001-2004
Gary R Lechte	2004-2011
John Connellan	2011-2017
Cameron Fisher	2017-current

SECRETARIES

E I F Halley	1968
D Scroggie	1968-1978
I D Scroggie	1978-2004
R Jennings	2004-current

TREASURERS

F Spottiswood	1968
J H Thomson	1969-1971
Judge A M Fraser	1971
J H Thomson	1972-1986
H A Evans	1987-1993
M Kostos	1994-1998
D Rowe	1999-2002
R Jennings	2003
I D Scroggie	2004-2008
F Bayne	2009-current

HONORARY Membership of the Thoroughbred Club was handed to the chairman of the Melbourne Racing Club (Victoria Amateur Turf Club) when giving the traditional toast to the Caulfield Cup on the eve of the great race.

The first to receive that honour was Sir Rupert Clarke in 1976. The club then bestowed Honorary Membership to the chairmen of the three principal clubs and other leading administrators and racing identities.

Others to receive it were VATC (MRC) chairman Rupert Steele, Peter Lawrence, Peter Young, Kevin Hayes and Mike Symonds (John Dillion was a member); Victoria Racing Club chairmen Sir Alec Creswick, Peter Armytage, David Bourke, Andrew Ramsden, Rod Fitzroy, Michael Burn and Amanda Elliott; Moonee Valley chairmen Ian MacDonald, Bill Stutt, Geoff Torney, Don Abell, Norman Carlyon, Bob Scarborough and Don Casboult; Ministers for Racing Brian Dixon, Neil Trezise and Tom Reynolds; champion trainer Bart Cummings; the Director of Racing and Gaming Phil Power; then Melbourne Lord Mayor Ron Walker; Father John Brosnan; Carlton and United Beverages boss Neil Grant; media guru Bill Collins; UK racing manager for Juddmonte Farm Lord Teddy Grimthorpe, media men Bruce Clark and Rod Nicholson and RVL chief steward Terry Bailey, and in 2018, Laurie Larmer, Ron Hutchison and Craig Willis.

THOROUGHBRED CLUB OF AUSTRALIA

(Incorporated 13th January 1988)

The formation meeting of the inaugural members took place at the Hotel Australia on January 9, 1968, when 13 prominent racing identities gathered to discuss the idea of a club to promote thoroughbred racing.

Those who attended this meeting were W. J. (Bill) Adams, F. (Frank) Cayley, W. C. (Warrick) Cayley, H. A. (Harold) Hall, E. I. F. (Ern) Halley, D. H. (Harold) Macknamara, F. (Frank) Reid, G. M. (Gordon) Skuce, F. (Fred) Spottiswood, W. G. (Glenn) Stott, J. H. (Bunny) Thomson, K. F. (Ken) Cox and F. L. (Fred) Norris.

The first documented formal meeting took place a couple of months later — on March 26 — when office bearers were elected.

Hal Hall became the inaugural president, with Warrick Cayley the vice-president, Ern Halley the secretary and Fred Spottiswood the treasurer.

That foursome formed the bulk of the committee alongside Frank Reid and Bunny Thomson.

The committee decided to invite R. S. (Robert) Dabscheck, W. W. (Bill) Cockram, and T. R. (Tom) Trevaskis into the club, while installing an initial membership ceiling of 20 members.

At the next meeting on April 23, E.D. (Ted) Mayes was invited to join, taking the number of members to 17.

Two important developments evolved at the following meeting on June 18 when Dave Scroggie, who was a guest of the club from the outset, took over as always intended as Honorary Secretary from Ern Halley, and Tom Travaskis was commissioned to organise a suitable club tie.

The appointment of Scroggie began a vital and productive period for the club. He was secretary for 10 years until his death in 1979, when his son Ian took over for the next 26 years. In all, the club has prospered from the efforts of only four secretaries, with Dave (10 years), Ian (26 years) and the incumbent Roger Jennings (14 years) holding the reins for all but six months of the club's first 50 years.

"Dad was always the choice to be club secretary and he took over within months of the inaugural meeting. He hadn't attended that first gathering but he was in the secretary's chair by June of 1968," Ian Scroggie explained.

"He attended as the guest of Glenn Stott and Ted Mayes, who owned Arnott's Chips.

"He was the secretary who led the club through the first decade of its development, but he died of cancer in 1979.

"I had been doing a lot of paperwork for him, and even attending a lot of meetings in the early 1970s. I was just filling in while dad was giving instructions from his hospital bed.

"When he died, I got all the papers together and took them to Henry Harrison, who promptly said I was to become the honorary secretary 'until I find someone'. He never tried to get anybody else and I just took over where dad had left off.

"Over time some people thought I had too much power, but all I was doing was what Henry wanted. So, when there was a push by a splinter group to get rid of me in the mid-1980s, Henry became as angry as I'd ever seen him. He rarely swore but he said some unprintable words that day.

"Henry simply stepped in, made my prospective challenger Bob Nunn the secretary of the Thoroughbred Racehorse Owners' Association, which we had formulated in 1974, and of which he was chairman for six years, and left it at that. Nunn was a magistrate and more into football than racing and he didn't survive long at TROA.

"Yet again, Henry had his way. The Thoroughbred Club was his baby and he loved it — and nobody was going to upset the applecart if he could help it.

"In those early days the club was made up of wealthy, astute businessmen who had some time on their hands. Many were senior officials at race clubs, others were prominent breeders and all were major horse owners. That they had a ceiling of only 20 members shows how exclusive the club was. Someone had to die or leave the club for a replacement to be included.

"Later the ceiling was raised to 40, and by 1982 it was 55. Everything that the club did was paid for by members. There was no sponsorship, so you needed a sizeable financial base to get membership, and to retain it.

"The club was incorporated in 1988 because someone else was trying to use the Thoroughbred Club to promote their business. They advertised in the

Sporting Globe for people to join the Thoroughbred Club, which had nothing to do with us. So, we lodged the papers under the Incorporation Act to ensure nobody else could use it."

THE decision to produce a club tie has, of course, remained significant for the club to this day.

Tom Trevaskis had a tie designed that was a simple dark navy blue with gold stripes with TC embroidered front and centre. It was introduced in time for the first annual Caulfield Cup eve luncheon in October of 1968.

The late Vic Peters picked out the embroidery, which, he claimed much to his chagrin, that his wife didn't like!

Multiple varieties of the club tie, both shapes and designs, were introduced over the decades. However, for the late Keith Southwick the original was the best — he wore the same model throughout his four decades of membership.

The late Merv Brown generously funded the full cost of club ties during his association with the Club. He also came to the fore when the club's original small banner was misplaced when in storage at the Hotel Australia. He funded and had manufactured a much larger one.

Fines for not wearing your club tie could be financially painful. Nick Columb discovered that after his super filly Imposera won the Thoroughbred Club Stakes in 1987.

"Henry and I noticed him without his club tie and Henry immediately confronted him and informed him he was fined $500."

Nick offered the lame excuse that he had preferred to wear his "lucky tie" rather than the club tie, but before he could spit out the rest of his explanation Henry jumped in.

"Don't you dare carry on with this or I will seriously consider doubling his fine!" Nick shut up, flicked his "lucky tie" between his fingers and paid up.

Fines were particularly significant in the early years of Harrison's reign. The toughest was imposed upon future president Gary Lechte, then an entrepreneurial Frankston car salesman.

Lechte decided to use the Thoroughbred Club Caulfield Cup eve luncheon to promote his business, which was a shrewd move given more than 500 people attended the popular function.

In 1994 he placed footballs, displaying his business, on all 50 tables. Harrison was unamused. When he rose to speak he asked Lechte to also stand and told him he was delighted that he had his bank manager with him, because he had decided to impose a $1000 fine for the "unsanctioned" publicity stunt and "unauthorised use of facilities."

"I couldn't wait to pay up, which I did by cheque the next day, because I reckon I got $10,000 of free publicity for the football promotion, and double that when Henry made such a big deal of it at the function!" Lechte said.

"I remember I stood up like a little schoolboy when Henry called me out. I did it not only to promote my businesses, but to promote Fraar who was going to stud. He won the 1993 Caulfield Cup and was heading to my stud the following year (1994) and I wanted everyone to know.

"So, I'd organised showbags for everyone who attended, containing caps advertising Fraar and grass from the Caulfield race course and other goodies. Then I added a white football on every table with Gary Lechte Toyota, Berwick Nissan and Berwick Jeep stamped all over them! People were fighting to decide who would claim the footy to take home."

While Lechte figured the stunt was a promotional bonanza, he did fear he had put himself on the wrong side of Harrison, which was a virtual death-wish at the Thoroughbred Club.

However, he quickly discovered that rather than being in the bad books, he was in the good books.

"Not long after Henry fined me that $1000, I realised that rather than having it in for me, he actually liked me. He told me he would like to race a horse with me. As it turned out, trainer Bevan Laming was at my farm and had a call that, basically, suggested a potential client wasn't going to come good with the funds for a horse he had bought in New Zealand. I asked how much it cost and when he said it was $20,000, adding that the horse had genuine potential, I bought in and split up shares with Henry and Geoff Dawson, Marty Godby and John

Wheatley, with Jenny Laming taking the other share," Lechte said.

"It turned out that Donnie Brasco was virtually unbeatable in heavy conditions (nine wins, four seconds and a third from 25 starts in those conditions) and he gave us all a heap of fun."

"Henry loved it," Lechte said. "Henry said the friendship and fun from being part of that horse was worth far more than the prizemoney."

From what could have been a swift parting of the ways, Lechte and Harrison developed a long and personal friendship and, over the journey, contributed 32 years as president of the Thoroughbred Club between them.

Nobody is immune from fines. When club president Cameron Fisher forgot to wear the club tie to a Thoroughbred Club race day at Caulfield in 2018, he was automatically fined $500.

THE club's early elders wanted to make an impact on the racing scene and decided to invite prominent members of the media to their next meeting in September of 1968.

The idea was to explain to the ilk of Jack Elliott from *The Herald*, Jack McPherson (*The Sun*), Ron Taylor (*Truth*), Tony Bourke (*The Age*) and Peter Lovett (*The Australian*) the reason for the inauguration of the club and its mission. The media became a vital part of the club's success. Elliott, the most fearsome racing writer over three decades at *The Herald*, later became a club member. To have him on-side was a huge bonus — to have him against you usually meant death by a thousand lashings, as he did when repeatedly degrading Caulfield as the VERY Amateur Turf Club.

Other key media folk to have an input into the club include broadcaster John Russell, Channel Seven supremo Ron Casey and ace race caller Bill Collins.

Casey, his sidekick and footy guru Lou Richards and Collins formed the most famous, decorated and talented trio of media folk in the nation.

Casey, a master communicator, conducted many interviews over the years and was a valued member of the Club from 1975 until his passing in 2000.

He was a radio presenter with 3DB from the late 1940s to the late 1970s, and covered sport around the globe, despite also being the station's sports director. He also joined HSV-7 in 1956 and was host of the famous *World Of Sport* program for 28 years. He became studio manager in 1969 and was general manager from 1972 until 1987, when the station was sold to the Fairfax Group.

On Australia Day 1995 he became the first personality to appear on Australian Pay-TV.

But it was his love of sport, his knowledge of such a variety of it, that made him a focal point at any Thoroughbred Club gathering.

He was involved in one way or another in football, cycling, boxing, racing, tennis and basketball. He was involved as a broadcaster at 10 Olympic Games, with Davis Cup tennis, cycling, world boxing titles and football.

There was virtually no sport that Casey could not discuss intimately and that made him a most popular club member. Many believe his greatest broadcasting moment came on radio, when in 1968 he described the world title fight between Lionel Rose and Fighting Harada in Tokyo. His most memorable interview also came from the world of boxing when, in the 1960s, he interviewed American legend Rocky Marciano on *World of Sport*.

His greatest moments in football came late in life when his beloved Kangaroos won the 1996 and 1999 AFL premierships when he was club president. He developed *TV Ringside* which produced two World and four Commonwealth champions and took boxing to a new audience.

Casey lived a full life and knew anybody who was anybody in Victoria. He was a member of the Kangaroos' Board between 1987-2000, and chairman from 1991-2000; he was a member of the Boxing Control Board; for seven years a member of the Harness Racing Board; a past president of the Carbine Club of which he was a member for 26 years; an associate member of the Sport Australia Hall of Fame; chairman of the Professional Boxing and Martial Arts Board of Victoria; a Committee Member of the Mornington Racing Club, an executive member of the Moonee Valley Racing Club and honorary member of the Victoria Club.

In his spare time, he was a founding member of VicHealth and was a board member for 12 years as well as being a life member of the Victorian Arts Centre.

He was awarded an MBE in 1984 and in 1989 received an Order of Australia award. He also was an inaugural inductee into the Australian Football Hall of Fame. The Melbourne Cricket Ground's media centre is called the Ron Casey Media Centre in his honour.

THAT flamboyant footy guru Lou Richards was a regular alongside Ron Casey was not surprising. Lou was a star at Channel 7, notably for *League Teams* and *World of Sport*, and Casey ran the television station.

Besides being close mates, Lou knew that being (permanently) on the right side of Casey was a passport to anything and everything at Channel 7. Although he was never a member of the Thoroughbred Club, he was a regular at major functions as Ron's guest.

Geoff Dawson said Lou was often the centre of attention, but one particular evening stood out.

"After the functions at the Southern Cross a group of us would head to a Chinese restaurant to carry on the frivolities. One night we sat Lou on the Lazy Susan and he spun around and around. By the end of it he couldn't stand up and didn't know where he was!" Dawson said. "He was a barrel of laughs and gave a lot of people a good time at his own expense."

Lou played 250 games for Collingwood between 1941 and 1955, captaining the club between 1952-55, which included the 1953 premiership.

However, he is more remembered for his wit and vivacity as a media entertainer, a trait he brought to the Thoroughbred Club.

THE third member of the trilogy was Bill Collins, a far more independent member of the Channel 7 crew, who was an honorary member of the Thoroughbred Club for a couple of decades given his master-of-ceremony duties.

He was the race broadcaster known as "The Accurate One" for his amazing ability to guarantee the listener was informed of how his wager was going and then nailing the winner and place-getters in the closest of finishes.

He was so good that his calls on radio station 3DB was used as a voice-over on Channel 7 race replays on *World Of Sport*. It was as if he was calling the race off the film, such was his accuracy. Yet his call was the live broadcast from the Saturday meeting, simply overlapping the visual recording to perfection.

As was the case with many radio personalities of the day, Bill wore multiple hats that included being the host of the entertainment program *Sunnyside Up*, for which he won a Logie Award in 1959, as well as making his television debut on HSV-7 on *The Penthouse Club* that televised harness racing.

His quick wit, horse racing knowledge and affable character made him one of the most popular master-of-ceremonies any club could enjoy.

Collins also was the first Australian race caller to work in the United States. South Africa also welcomed him with open arms, and he further enhanced his reputation with outstanding work on three English Derbies. He also called races in Hong Kong, New Zealand and Singapore.

He was so highly regarded in the industry that he frequently filled in for Ron Casey on *World Of Sport* for almost 20 years.

Besides racing and the media, Collins was elected chairman of the South Melbourne football club in 1981, restoring the club's viability.

He also filled duties for the Harness Racing Board in 1985 and 1986, the latter year being the highlight call of the Our Waverly Star and Bonecrusher clash in the Cox Plate when he uttered the famous line: "And Bone Crusher races into equine immortality."

Collins next served as chairman of the Greyhound Racing Control Board in 1987, by which time he had called a then record 34 Melbourne and Caulfield Cups. Bill was recognised for his contribution to radio and television by being awarded the Bert Wolf Award for Excellence in Journalism.

Club members regularly gleaned inside knowledge into race form and odds from Collins, and the astute also sought his advice on other sports.

What many may not know is that Collins called athletics at three Olympic Games: in Melbourne in 1956, Montreal in 1976 and Moscow in 1980.

He was awarded the Order of Australia Medal (OAM) in 1987 and was an inaugural inductee into the Australian Racing Hall of Fame. He called his last race on Easter Sunday of 1988 and died in 1997.

He enjoyed playing cards and smoking as much as he did the gallops, dogs and trots, and was a great entertainer who, for many years, set the mood at the Thoroughbred Club functions.

Members attending any function at Caulfield walk past his statue, sited just inside the members' gates, which is a fitting welcome.

PERHAPS fortunately for the club, the ilk of Casey, Collins and Richards were not around when the club was formed. As Ian Scroggie points out, there was no pretence about what the original membership intended — to be a lobby group to get their preferred candidates onto race club committees.

"This was evident from the initial mission statement, which coincided with the first annual Caulfield Cup eve luncheon on October 18 of 1968.

"The initial members were most influential people, all pretty much millionaires, and many of them on the Victoria Amateur Turf Club, Victoria Racing Club or Moonee Valley committees.

"Yet the very first mission statement, which was included on the official program at the Caulfield Cup eve function, contained these passages:

> *"Considerable publicity has been given to the Club since its inception and most of this is appreciated as being accurate. However, there is one aspect of the Club's activities which has been published, and which is inaccurate.*

"It has been suggested that the Club is 'a power group' set on getting its members seats on the Committee of Race Clubs. It was specifically written into the Rules of the Club on formation that the Club would not take part in or sponsor any candidate, member or otherwise, for a position on a Race Club Committee, nor permit any discussion thereon at our meetings.

"It must be appreciated, however, that Club Rules have no power to control individuals, and if any member of the Club does in fact stand for Race Club Committee election, then it is entirely the responsibility of the individual whether he wishes to help him or otherwise.

"There is no significance in the fact that since its formation, one member of the Club has been elected to the V.R.C Committee, and it would be surprising if in the future, other members don't offer themselves for election. The majority of our members have a very large stake in the Racing Industry, and it would seem they have some reason to consider Committee elections."

As Scroggie suggested, it was an extraordinary few passages for an official program. "And it was a nonsense. If you stood for a race club committee, you would be given a list of all members. It was common knowledge that Tom Trevaskis, who owned Trevola Robes, would have a gathering of TBC members attend his office, sit around a table and ring club members to solicit votes.

"There was nothing illegal about that, but for the Club to put out a statement on the program of its first Caulfield Cup eve function made a mockery of the mission statement.

"There was a meeting soon after to make several constitutional changes, the most significant of which was the exclusion of any member seeking to nominate for either the VATC or the VRC committee. This prompted several resignations, including that of dynamic businessman Ken Cox."

Cox was perhaps the most prominent breeder in Victoria as owner of Stockwell Stud, which he bought in 1957 on property at Digger's Rest. It was the epicentre of Victorian breeding, standing a host of notable stallions including the iconic Showdown, Comeram, Star Shower and Empryean.

Showdown, who stood at Stockwell Stud between 1966 and 1983, won two

Australian sires' premierships, produced 46 stakes winners including 13 at Group 1 level, and produced winners of the Golden Slipper, Blue Diamond, Oaks and Derby. So, it was a considerable blow when Ken Cox, among other VRC members with committee ambitions, resigned. He did so in October 1968, only nine months after the club started.

However, he re-joined in August 1976 when all the controversy died down. He had an immediate impact, winning the Thoroughbred Club Stakes with Happy Kitten in 1977, the first year the race was run at Caulfield.

When Showdown retired from stud duties in 1983, died and was buried at Stockwell Stud in 1985, Cox sold the stud.

He was guest speaker at several club luncheons, imparting his knowledge of the breeding industry.

Unsurprisingly, the contentious passages from the original mission statement were deleted by the following year, and it has remained unchanged for the next 49 years.

It reads:

> *To promote, foster and encourage closer co-operation and better business relations in the thoroughbred horse industry, to provide a forum for the discussion and interchange of ideas relating to the raising, breeding, racing and marketing of thoroughbred horses and to encourage public interest therein; to gather and disseminate such knowledge and information pertaining to the breeding, raising and racing of thoroughbred horses or interest and value to persons having a common interest therein; and in general to endeavour in every proper and lawful way to promote better business conditions in said industry."*

That certainly remains a mouthful today, and, with a bit of sub-editing, can be interpreted that the club aims to do everything possible to popularise our great sport for the benefit of all those interested in the industry. And have a lot fun doing it!

THE inaugural Caulfield Cup eve luncheon program contains a menu that may bring back memories for many. It read:

Seafood Cocktail
Roast Beef
Vegetables in Season
Apple Pie with Cream
Coffee

REIGNING Thoroughbred Club president Cameron Fisher can lay claim to setting at least one standard before his elevation to the top job: parking arrangements for those game enough to take a car to the Caulfield Cup eve luncheon at The Heath. "After yet another boozy Caulfield Cup eve luncheon I decided I was too intoxicated to drive home so I left my car at the track. It wasn't until the following morning, not long before the first race on Caulfield Cup day, that the Melbourne Racing Club chief executive Peter Sweeney rang and asked if I could kindly remove my Mercedes from the betting ring!

"Members were denied access to that area from then on, and understandably so," he recalled. Cameron, who took over as president in 2017, went to Thoroughbred Club luncheons for about seven years as a guest of Graeme Sampieri and then Jack Eastgate before being nominated by Tony Cavanagh, who was instrumental in getting him on the board at TROA, to become a member in 1996.

At that stage the club had a limit of 60 members and Cameron recalls attending lunches at the Southern Cross before re-organising car parking arrangements at Caulfield. Cameron's dramas were not restricted to car parking, as he explains a venture to Adelaide with his mate and trainer Brian Ralph that almost went horribly wrong.

"In 1989 during the pilot strike we drove to Adelaide where I backed our galloper Noble Talent with a few bookies and when the lovely animal saluted I was to collect $30,000. I asked the bookies for cheques, but they refused and instead insisted on paying me cash.

"Anyway, my wife and I hired a car as Ralphy was staying on in Adelaide and drove back to Ballarat. We decided to have dinner before turning in after a long day. But when we headed back to the motel unit, the police were there. The unit next to us had been raided and the police, once we told them about our big collect, realised the robbers had raided the wrong room.

"The robbers had tailed us all the way from Adelaide to Ballarat but what they didn't know was that I had stuffed all the money into a T-shirt and wrapped it around my stomach before going to dinner. It showed me just how careful you had to be when you won big, because a big loss can be just around the corner.

> "We put him in a trial under a different horse's name and, on his performance, he was a good thing"

"A couple of weeks later we returned to Adelaide, and this time we hired a plane. Despite our confidence, the horse didn't salute and all I can say is that the best ride our hoop Pat Trotter had all day was in the cockpit on the way home!"

Fisher, who was introduced to racehorse ownership by Les Cooper, who was a valuer whose horses were trained by Brian Ralph, had his biggest day on the punt in 1989 when he was only in his mid-20s.

"I was in the ownership of Raw Talent and he won his first start at Caulfield by about five lengths. We put him in a trial under a different horse's name and, on his performance, he was a good thing. I won $130,000 when he saluted and bought a hobby farm behind Hanging Rock with my parents.

"Unfortunately, the horse suffered from a heart strain so I gave him to Mike Hewson who had done wonders with Street Ruffian, who also had that problem. He won with him on the Friday and then again on the Monday and I still remember the words of a committeeman at Pakenham, "Winning is the best fun a man can have with his pants on!""

Fisher said he has owned more than 100 horses along the journey, starting in 1985 at the age of 23 with Indeed I Do which finished third in the Debutante Stakes 32 years ago.

"I have had two winners of the Geelong Derby — Prince Miasma with Rod Menzies in 1996 — and Extra Choice with Mark Pilkington and others including AFL boss Gillon McLachlan in 2015 — and they both ran in the Victoria Derby. I've also had Oaks runners but the best result I've enjoyed is at Listed level."

Fisher's relationship with Rod Menzies is an extraordinary tale.

"I was at a Thoroughbred Club luncheon when a work colleague of Rod said I should meet him because we both had an interest in horse ownership. He rang Rod and told him to get into his car and head to an address in Elizabeth Street in Elsternwick. He didn't have to go far — he lived directly opposite me!

"And to top it off, my next-door neighbour was club member Peter Maher.

"Anyway, I linked up with Rod in horse ownership and we had a two-year-old making his debut one day and decided to have a meeting to devise the best way to make a dollar. We were going to set up the big sting — from a McDonald's outlet!

"We backed the second favourite for plenty so that the price of our horse drifted considerably and then waited for the big sting to land us the loot.

"Well, we ran unplaced and the only consolation was that the second favourite we had backed actually won. At least we made a little out of our grandiose plan!

"Rod Menzies has been a great mate and a tremendous contributor to the Thoroughbred Club. I remember one venture between us that didn't last — art auctioning. Rod asked me to be the co auctioneer at the Deutscher-Menzies inaugural art auction which was rather different to real estate auctioning. There were unusual challenges such as the pronunciation of Aboriginal artists. And on a couple of occasions I inadvertently referred to telephone bids as 'telephone bets'…

"Suffice it to say my art auctioning days were short lived.

"But I was the agent who auctioned one of Rod's multimillion dollar homes, the art dealer's abode before he moved into a far bigger and more luxurious home. It was only a launching pad for him."

Indeed, it was. Menzies bought Stonnington for $18 million — the highest priced paid at that time for a Melbourne house — in August of 2007 — and converted it into a private home that housed his extensive art collection, including works by Brett Whiteley, John Olsen and Arthur Boyd.

He held functions for club members at Stonnington, the heritage-listed mansion with adjoining gatehouse on 1.2 hectares of land.

"It is the same residence that housed Victoria's governors between 1901 and 1931 and has entertained guests including Dame Nellie Melba and the Duke and Duchess of York (King George VI and Queen Elizabeth), so Thoroughbred Club members were in good company!" Cameron said.

Rod Menzies is best known as the chairman and managing director of two of Australia's largest auction houses — Deutscher-Menzies and the Sydney-based Lawson-Menzies, and at the time he bought Stonnington his investments in horseracing, real estate and contract cleaning reportedly were turning over more than $200 million a year.

"It opened a world of opportunities"

He recently sold Stonnington for a Victorian record price of $52 million.

Menzies has raced horses for half-a-century and is passionate about two-year-olds, although he did own 2003 Queensland Derby winner Half Hennessey, who bolted in by six lengths.

Fisher recalls with a chuckle being invited to the weekly Friday lunches alongside a couple of dozen club members.

"The group had decided they wanted to have more connection than just a monthly meeting, so they met every Friday afternoon at the Royal South Yarra tennis club. It was a good mix of people, including Des Rowe and Fred Bayne and yours truly among as many as of two dozen of us.

"They called it the Group One Club, as most of them had had Group 1 winners. However, Henry Harrison initially saw it as a potential breakaway group and a threat to the Thoroughbred Club. It was funny, in retrospect, because the Friday luncheon group was, in fact, cementing friendships which started and were to continue at the Thoroughbred Club.

"From my point of view, for a young man to be mingling with top businessmen, owners and breeders and all kinds of champion sports people was just amazing. It opened a world of opportunities. I recall the first photo shoot I was involved in with all the other club members: there I was standing next to George Smorgon, the patriarch of one of Melbourne's most prominent families. Not only was he an exceptional businessman, he owned (with Nick Column) the 1985 Caulfield Cup winner Tristarc and that year's Australasian Oaks winner Centaurea.

"He was a marvellous person to be associated with in any way, and he was sadly missed when he died in 2004," Fisher said.

Fisher said club members were generous and always on the lookout to help others, even it was just a little ego boost.

"On March 9 last year (2017) the club had a night at the Sandown greyhounds — it happened to be my birthday — and former club president Geoff Dawson named one of the races the 'Happy Birthday Cameron handicap'.

"That is only one small example of the great camaraderie that envelops this club. To be a member is worth its weight in gold," Fisher said.

GARY LECHTE is one of the great characters, and contributors, in the history of the Thoroughbred Club.

Over the journey he has been chairman (2004-11), inducted as a life member in 2015, a social organiser, entrepreneur, winner of the Thoroughbred Club Owners award in 1997 and 2018 and, without doubt, a funster.

He's boasted Group 1 winners; a 100/1 shot city winner; stood a Melbourne Cup and a Caulfield Cup winner at his stud; is an outstanding piano-accordionist and plays the piano too. He bought John Cleese's car in the US and he knows the Osborne family, and was responsible for getting Barry Humphries to perform as Sir Les Patterson at a Thoroughbred Club luncheon.

Along the way he has been a bookie, a super successful car salesman, and a man versatile enough to take over the controls of a plane when the pilot blacked out. He could even organise Santa to arrive by helicopter at his Dromana property to entertain the kids at the Thoroughbred Club Christmas party.

Lechte believes his involvement with the Thoroughbred Club has given him unbridled pleasure. But, equally, he has given Thoroughbred Club members unlimited time and effort to ensure they have a fun time.

The Lechte story in racing began at an early age.

"My uncle, Peter Maddern, was a bookmaker who worked alongside Graeme Sampieri and Mark Read.

"I learned all about bookmaking and from 1972-1974 I ran a book at Huntingdale High. Even the teachers bet with me!

"I wrote Ranwick on top of one page of bets. I couldn't spell but I sure could count!"

"I've still got the books from those days. I wrote Ranwick on top of one page of bets. I couldn't spell but I sure could count! The kids would bet in 20c and 50c, and I even had tickets made up to make it official.

"I was heading for a hiding in the Caulfield Cup of 1973 but fortunately Swell Time saluted and it was a skinner.

"Then I got a bookie's clerk license in 1975 — at the cost of $2 — and worked with uncle Peter for five years running bets, betting back, pencilling and anything that would help earn a quid."

John Connellan knows that Lechte has racing in his veins. In fact, he relates the time he rang Ross Stevenson and Hamish McLachlan on their *That's Racing* program on Racing.com to tell them about Lechte for their segment called "You know you are addicted to racing when…"

"They told stories about when you are driving your car and you say to you wife you are one-out and one-back or that you are going to take the rails run.

"So, I told them of the day that Lechte took David Hayes to lunch at the Flower Drum and when the Cloudy Bay sav blanc arrived he told the waiter to 'put its full sister on ice.' Now that's an addiction to racing!" Connellan said.

Lechte joined the CBA bank at Oakleigh and recalls how he had to attend shooting practice. "It is hard to believe now, but everyone had a black revolver, loaded, under the counter."

Then one day he saw the annual pay slip of the bank manager and realised he would never get rich sticking with the bank.

"I saw an advertisement for Bayside Holden which said you could earn a bundle, with a car and fuel supplied.

"When I arrived, I earned $146 for the week as basic pay. But I sold 11 cars that week and earned $980 in commission, giving me a week's wage of $1128. That was in 1977 and was a lot of money!

"I soon started Cheltenham Nissan on the Nepean Highway and made millions out of its sale. I was doing good business but selling cars helped cash flow but didn't make you rich. Then I was offered a fabulous sum to sell the business. It included the property, which I owned, and the offer was a real lot of money in those days and just too good to refuse. As it turned out, I did a swap with the buyer, taking over his Berwick business, getting his property, as well as pocketing a small fortune."

Lechte rarely tells the tale of the time, at age 35, he took control of a float plane at Port Douglas when the pilot blacked out.

He was sitting beside the pilot of the Beaver plane when, about 15 minutes after take-off, the pilot became violently ill and lost consciousness.

Lechte, who had taken flying lessons at Moorabbin a few years earlier, flew the plane for about 50 seconds and was preparing to land on water after it plunged 200m immediately the pilot lost control.

Lechte enjoyed Group 1 success with Cut Up Rough in the 1997 VicHealth Cup at Caulfield, trained by Peter Hayes and ridden by Steven King.

It was an overdue success after he was beaten by Our Maizcay by a nostril in the feature two years earlier. He also was a certainty beaten in a roughhouse Newmarket Handicap the same year, was unlucky in the Manikato in 1997, and ran into Saintly when second in the Group 1 Orr Stakes of 1997.

He had to wait until He's Our Rokkii won the Toorak Handicap in 2016 to notch his next Group 1 winner, a success he shared with club member Mark Pilkington, Darren Thomas and Jon Lechte.

However, he still recalls vividly his "best Group 1 placing" which involved Clever Zoe. "As a two-year-old she contested the Lightning Stakes in 1992 and led a cracking field by four lengths, only to be run down by the champion Schillaci in record time.

"The best thing to come out of that race was my long friendship with the great Dr Alan Bell."

In 2010 Lechte sold his thoroughbred stud Delamere in Moorooduc Road in Dromana which he had owned for 20 years. It meant the dispersal of many of the items Lechte had accumulated, including his items from his lifelong passion for classic American cars, racehorses and significant sporting memorabilia.

The 100 hectares homestead had enabled him to indulge all three pursuits — horses, "big Yank tanks" and his memorabilia.

Delamere itself was famous for some of the champion racehorses that have stood there at stud. They included 1986 Melbourne Cup winner At Talaq (owned by racing giant Dubai's Sheik Hamdan Bin Rashid Al Maktoum) who died of a heart attack and is buried on the property, and the 1993 Caulfield Cup winner Fraar, which Gary purchased with the late Colin Hayes.

Lechte put under the hammer that day a 1959 Chevrolet four-door hardtop with 35,000 miles, original interior, registration and contract of sale papers — along with two 1959 left-hand drive Buicks.

"The Chevrolet cost $US2190 when brand new," Gary said. "One of the Buicks (an ex funeral car) is a black Electra 225, named after the length of the vehicle." The other is a red La Sabre Coupe with a white roof in showroom condition that he bought in Seattle and drove down the United States west coast to Los Angeles.

The sporting memorabilia, some of it from the old Victorian Club in Queen Street, included the club's original grand piano, an early photo of billiard great Walter Lindrum and several early horse racing prints. Other sporting items included a board devoted to Phar Lap's 1930 racing victories and a tote board from the same era signed by J. Baker, the first jockey to ride the legendary Red Terror to victory. Also on offer were the original silks from Rising Fast's 1954 Melbourne Cup win along with those worn by Jim Cassidy the day he rode Might and Power to victory in the 1997 version of the race.

On a more personal note, there was a signed framed Bill Clinton portrait and baseball bat that Gary obtained during a 2002 Australian dinner the president attended, and photographs and signatures of nine presidents from John F. Kennedy to George Bush senior.

A mahogany banquet dining setting with 12 chairs, a 22-carat gold gilded French display cabinet, heavy oak sideboard and French bergere armchairs, a Keogh and Bourne 40-year collection of Royal Worcester including pieces by George Owen and Charles Baldwyn were other amazing items that Lechte sold.

GEOFF DAWSON came to know Henry Harrison by chance. Yet he worked for him, married his daughter and ended up club president in Henry's footsteps.

"I actually joined the club at the same time as Henry, having been nominated by John Russell in 1972," he recalled.

"I first met Henry at the trots when I was running around bets and he was working for a bookie.

"It turned out we both lived in Caulfield and he had a beautiful daughter, Loretta, whom I eventually married.

"Henry was doing some SP-betting and I helped him write bets and we ended up good mates," he said.

Dawson said his relationship with Henry was a lot of fun, in many ways unlike the usual father-in-law and son-in-law relationship.

"We dedicated ourselves to having as good a time as we possibly could"

"Henry wasn't at the Thoroughbred Club very long before he took over. He did a wonderful job and got the club to where it is today.

"I was by his side almost all the way. We were involved in the club together during his 25 years as president, and he supported me when I took over as president a couple of years after he retired.

"We were together at the greyhounds — again, I followed him in as president. We were together at the farm, and in horse ownership together. It was a wonderful relationship," he said.

"I spent three years as president and had great fun. We always took entertainment very seriously because besides being a club that fosters interest and involvement in thoroughbred racing, we also dedicated ourselves to having as good a time as we possibly could.

"And we loved owning a winner. Gary Lechte put us in Donnie Brasco, and Skinny Saunders bought All Shot for Henry. He won two William Reid Stakes, in 1973 and '74, and was runner-up in another.

"I owned Smokey Dark which was trained by Skinny Saunders and won 14 races. At one stage Henry suggested that we should run our own farm at Tyabb. We then moved to Pearcedale on 162 acres. We had plenty of horses on the property and we held Christmas parties, which were great fun for everybody, with all the food and drink and entertainment first-class."

One of the most cherished keepsakes Dawson has from the Thoroughbred Club is a ship's bell, which came via Henry Harrison from Neville Stibbard, who presented it to him at the AGM in July of 1984.

Stibbard was a deeply-involved member of the Thoroughbred Club, and, besides his outside work and devotion to the South Melbourne Football Club as club recruiter, he was always looking for ways to help.

In a spontaneous gesture, he presented club president Harrison with a magnificently restored, polished, engraved and suitably-mounted ships bell."

He surprised all bar secretary Ian Scroggie with the off-the-agenda presentation at a monthly meeting.

Stibbard thought the bell would assist the president in bringing meetings to order should they get out of control.

Dawson, who has the ship's bell in pride of place at his home, said it is one of his prized possessions.

JOHN CONNELLAN has contributed so much to the Thoroughbred Club but even he will consider his crowning glory was organising the club's gala 50th anniversary party at Rippon Lea in March of 2018.

As several members opined, it was the stuff of Hollywood — champagne served by a lovely lass in a dolly varden (champagne glasses lined up in her bouffant panniers dress), a couple of attractive lace-clad trapeze artists, a lady in the huge champagne glass who was the centre of incessant photos, a shoe-shiner for the men and a make-up artist for the ladies, not to mention fabulous food and unlimited drink, all at the heritage-listed historic house and gardens in Elsternwick.

Upon entering the wrought-iron front gates, guests were greeted by musicians, entertained by a bookie along the driveway before being met by a newshound and photographer who directed people along the garden path to the back of the mansion, where you were trumpeted in and announced to the gathering. Then it was down to the drinking and mingling, wining and dining, laughing and entertainment as men sporting black ties and ladies in their finery overlooked the manicured gardens from the 1868-built historic house.

Connellan has a penchant for entertaining. While president of the Thoroughbred Club between 2011 and 2017, he insisted on telling the latest joke while giving his presidential address at the Caulfield Cup eve luncheon.

That should come as no surprise as Connellan considered becoming a professional stand-up comedian.

"I had a period some years back when I thought I either got myself an agent and did it seriously or just continued to tell jokes for the fun of it. I decided to just have fun," he said.

"It all started back in the early 1980s. I was the state junior cross-country champion, and second only to Rob de Castella in Australia. Anyway, I was nominated to contest the inaugural Sydney to Melbourne Ultramarathon in 1983 and, with Chris Wardlaw as my manager, I ran in that as well as the following year. It would never have gained much notoriety except that the old potato farmer Cliff Young won it.

"That led to sportsmen's nights and then, because of my business operations, to business motivational talks, always with humour involved.

"Having a laugh is such great fun and getting people to laugh is wonderful. I've spoken for 15 minutes before almost every home game of the Sorrento Football Club for the past four years and never told the same joke twice.

"I just love entertaining people."

He also has MC'd functions at Kew Golf Club and other golfing events, combining two of his passions.

He joins mates Rod Fitzroy, Colin Little, Graeme Sampieri and others on an annual golfing tour of Vietnam. It was on a recent trip they decided to buy a young galloper, to be trained by Little. On ANZAC Day of 2018, the two-year-old colt Vassilator won the Listed Anzac Day Stakes at Flemington at only his third start — at $101.

Connellan and all involved laughed all the way to the bank and buttered up in a $100,000 race at Headquarters three weeks later.

Connellan has owned half-a-dozen hotels during his time. He bought the Ranges in Gembrook, the Sarah Sands in Brunswick which he converted into Bridie O'Reilly's, The Fleece in South Melbourne, The Kensington in North Melbourne, the Hollyford Hotel in Carlton and the Racecourse Hotel in Caulfield.

However, his prime business for almost five decades has been building. He established Connellan Industries in 1980 with an emphasis on commercial refurbishment and restoration including shop fit-outs across the nation, executive boardrooms and sensitive laboratories. The group has restored warehouses, resorts, schools and universities, and even branched out into ship cabins, hospitals, airports and sound studios.

But in 2004 he fulfilled a vision to resurrect the SkyHigh Restaurant at Mount Dandenong, which had been closed for eight years with the site left to languish, unloved and unwanted.

He created a world-class tourist attraction and function centre, which 14 years later attracts almost 500,000 visitors a year.

He improved the site with extra car-park facilities, disabled access, barbecues and picnic areas, viewing platforms, magnificent gardens and walks, a souvenir/gift shop and the new SkyHigh Maze. The building provides great access to the stunning views that sweep across Mornington Peninsula and Port Phillip Bay to the You Yangs on the Southern horizon.

"I spent $4 million doing it up and it now rates in the Top 10 tourist sites in Victoria," he said proudly.

"Then about three years ago I spent $1 million buying and doing up an old shed in the National Rhododendron Gardens called Mist @ Olinda.

"I knew a bit about hospitality because of my involvement in pubs, and as an off-shoot of this I ended up in the catering business as well.

"I initially put in a young manager and worked a couple of days with him to show him the ropes. But after four years he had an offer to go elsewhere. We had an understanding that we would meet every six months for a coffee and when we first met he was none too happy with his new employer.

"I suggested he start his own business, but he said he didn't have the money or the expertise. So, I financed him and gave him my experience and we went into a catering business together. Now Sean Robertson and I have been together for about eight years and we cater for all sorts of outlets, including the Healesville racecourse and function centres across Melbourne."

Connellan, who was nominated for the Thoroughbred Club by Graeme Sampieri, has a background in racing. His uncle Leon Lachal was secretary of the Sydney Turf Club for 13 years and was among the architects involved in the inaugural Golden Slipper Stakes in 1957, won by Todman, as well as being recognised as one of the main influencers in introducing starting stalls. The Victoria Racing Club recruited him in 1960 and he spent 10 years as secretary until his retirement in 1970.

Connellan remembers his uncle with awe.

"I remember going to the races and dreaming that we would run into Uncle Leon and he would invite us to the committee room. Well, one day my brother and I were wandering through the betting ring and we saw him walking towards us. We both yelled 'hello uncle Leon' and he said hello boys and just kept walking straight past us!

"He was such an imposing person. Besides being the secretary of this huge racing club, he was a decorated with the CBE for his time as an Air Commodore in the RAAF."

Connellan has been involved in racing and breeding for almost 30 years. With club members Ed McKeon and Harvey O'Neill, he won the Group 2 Herbert Power Stakes with Yakama and finished eighth in the 2003 Melbourne Cup behind Makybe Diva.

Another galloper he bred, Ascana, won the 2001 Moe Cup before being runner-up in the Werribee Cup and the Group 2 Queen Elizabeth Stakes.

"I think I was in the Thoroughbred Club for six years before I joined the committee and after another six years Gary Lechte announced he was standing down and he nominated me as his successor. I took over in 2011 and spent six great years as president and remain on the committee today.

"This is a wonderful club, packed with wonderful people, with racing the common factor.

"You just cannot buy the friendships you make at the Thoroughbred Club"

"You just cannot buy the friendships you make at the Thoroughbred Club. People come from all walks of life and they have vastly different backgrounds and professions but they all love racing, and they all enjoy a good time."

For once, he was not joking.

FRED BAYNE was honoured with Life Membership of the Thoroughbred Club in 2018 after 38 years of dedicated service.

Bayne was a regular guest of Geoff Dawson since the club began and became a member in September of 1980.

He joined the committee 28 years ago, has served as vice-president and, for the past decade, he has been charged with one of the most important tasks at the club — looking after the finances!

The now retired pharmacist from the Mornington Peninsula has been treasurer since 2009 and has ensured the club can afford the lavish functions to which it has become accustomed.

Always one to enjoy a drink and a chat, Bayne enjoys mingling with fellow club members and their guests as much today as he did 50 years ago.

"The early days were great and, like now for many, they became long nights every time we met," he recalls.

"Besides club meetings at the Southern Cross, Leonda and later at

Caulfield racecourse, we had great dinner dances, yachting adventures, golf days and Christmas parties. Henry Harrison entertained about 150 members and their families at his farm at Tyabb for Christmas and again when he moved to Devon Meadows. Young David (Harrison) had a motorbike on the property and quite a few of the blokes fancied themselves and went for a spin, which was more than amusing.

"Henry had some quality horses on his property, including All Shot. It was fantastic to look at the horses and enjoy Christmas on a delightful property with all the club mates.

"Then Gary Lechte took over and entertained us at his Delamere Stud at Mornington. And we had some great days at the Caulfield racecourse as well as the Hyatt in the city. We somehow always found a great venue to enjoy the festive season.

"We also enjoyed an annual golf day, playing at Kew, Keysborough and Sorrento, which Tony Ongarello organised, from the 1990s. We also had a competition day against the Carbine Club which ran for about six years from 2005, but unfortunately the Carbine Club couldn't muster the numbers in the end and that faded."

Bayne insists the number of wonderful people he has encountered over the decades at the Thoroughbred Club is what he cherishes most.

"That started from the very first club function I attended. I was placed next to Sir Stanley Leighton and we chatted amicable about all manner of topics, including horses. I mentioned that I owned a capable galloper named Mannered, who won several races in town.

"Anyway, two years later we were seated at the same table again, and Sir Stanley asked me how Mannered was going. For such an important man with so many interests in his life, it was wonderful that he not only remembered me, but my horse!

"He was a fascinating character, who lived with Lord Derby in England. His tales from those days were priceless.

"He lived in St Kilda and had, as they said at the time, a house keeper. He was a member for a long time and one of the first real characters I chanced upon. He owned Mornmoot Stud at Whittlesea, where the great Century was foaled and is buried. His son David remains a club member.

"Another great character was Jack Eastgate, who owned the champion Beau Zam and the smart filly Kapchat.

"But, boy, did he make up for his early disappointments!"

"He kept telling us that he owned 30 horses without ever having a winner until Beau Zam came along. But, boy, did he make up for his early disappointments!"

He certainly did. Beau Zam won the Group 2 Hill Stakes (1750m) at Rosehill and the Group 1 Spring Championship Stakes (2000m) at Randwick and then was runner-up by only a half head to Lord Reims in the 1987 Caulfield Cup on a bog Heavy 10 track at his next start — as a three-year-old.

He was trained by Bart Cummings and went on to be a champion and was named the Australian Racehorse of the Year in 1987/88. And for good reason. Besides the three wins mentioned above, he won five races on the trots as a three-year-old later that season, involving the Group 1 Segenhoe Stakes (2000m) by five lengths and Group 1 Tancred Stakes (2400m) by five-and-a-half lengths at Rosehill, the 1988 AJC Derby (2400m) at Randwick by five-and-a-half lengths and the Group 2 AJC St Leger (2800m) by a staggering 9.8 lengths. He then won the Queen Elizabeth Stakes (2000m) in Canberra in front of Her Majesty, beating Bonecrusher by a head with Dandy Andy seven lengths away in third.

The following season he won the Group 2 Apollo Stakes (1400m) and the Group 1 Segenhoe Stakes again by five-and-a-quarter lengths.

He ended his career in 1989 with a staggering $2,388,675 in prizemoney, being the first Australian horse to win more than $2 million. That was a huge sum in that era, and he retired with a record of 11 wins and seven placings from 28 starts.

Kapchat was a wonderful filly. She won six of her 15 starts (with five seconds) and collected more than $500,000 in prizemoney in the early 1990s. She won the Group 1 Winfield Stakes at Rosehill and was beaten only three-quarters of a length in the 1993 Thousand Guineas at Caulfield by Arborea.

"I suppose he had plenty of reasons to always be smiling after Beau Zam. However, it was just his nature to have a good time.

"I remember one day when Sir Rupert Steele was rambling on at a luncheon and people were starting to talk and fidget, so Jack jumped to his feet and shouted: "Prey silence for Sir Rupert!"

"Another member took it upon himself to take Jack off at every opportunity, yelling out at any time and in any place: "Prey silence for Sir Rupert." Jack loved it.

"Then there was Kevin Heffernan, a larger-than-life character. He was a VATC and MRC committeeman who owned many successful horses and a great sense of humour.

"He died in 2012 and is remembered annually via the Kevin Heffernan Stakes, run at Caulfield. His biggest win as an owner was Gold Trump, who was trained by Bart Cummings, in the 1990 Newmarket Handicap."

Bayne has close connections with club members, even away from Thoroughbred Club activities.

"For the past 25 years a group of us have had lunch every Friday at the Royal South Yarra Tennis Club. We started with about 18 but that number now is down to only eight with many passing on or moving away.

"Tony Ongarello always attends. He did so much for the club. He was on the committee for a time, organised the very popular sweep at the Caulfield Cup eve luncheon, as well as golf days.

"Of course, he is best remembered as the last League footballer to score a goal with a place kick. He actually kicked two late place kick goals in Fitzroy's narrow loss to Geelong in 1955 at the Brunswick Street Oval," Bayne recalled.

Ongarello, who later was a regular on ABC television football panels in the 1960s and 1970s, was Fitzroy's leading goalkicker in 1952, 1956 and 1958.

Bayne also has fond memories of his days with Michael Kostos, who celebrated his 92nd birthday in March of 2018.

"He was club treasurer for five years in the 1990s. He joined about the same time as me when the club was in its infancy. He was involved in the timber trade and had many horses with Bart Cummings. The best horse he owned was Swick, who won the Group 3 Sandown Stakes in 2006, the Group 2 Salinger Stakes at

Flemington in 2007 and then, in early 2008, was beaten a neck by Apache Cat in the Lightning Stakes.

"But his biggest win was in the Group 1 Patinack Classic down the Flemington straight, beating Turffontein, in the spring of 2008."

"He has been a great club member, organising Christmas functions for us at the Hyatt over the years.

"And he loved the Melbourne Football Club as much as he loved his racing. He was the No 1 ticketholder for many years and had been on the club's coterie since it started. A great character.

"So too was Tom Trevaskis. He nominated me for membership at the Club. He owned Monameith Stud and was a part-owner of the great Century.

(The story goes that Trevaskis named the star sprinter Century only because he had been knocked back 99 times with other names for the colt by the Registrar.)

Century, who won the 1973 Group 1 Newmarket Handicap, went on to be the sire of Rubiton.

"Tom was vice-president of the club for a time and always captivated people with his yarns on wrestling. He won gold in the welterweight division at the 1938 Empire (now Commonwealth) Games and made his living with the very successful clothing business, Trevola Robes."

Bayne has fond memories of many club members and loves mingling with the "new chums" as he carefully plots the financial future of the club.

JOHN DILLON is one of the Thoroughbred Club's most influential members, a past president between 1999 and 2001 and a life member since 2008.

In fact, according to his great mate and distinguished member Craig Dunn, Dillon was the only man capable of influencing iron-fisted president Henry Harrison in vital matters.

"That was evident on two important occasions," Dunn recalled. "John was a confidante of Henry, who had great respect for him. Henry was a great mate of John's father Sir John and John not only worked as legal counsel for the Sandown greyhounds, he also was like a son to Henry.

"So, when Henry was getting on in years and club members were muttering about a succession plan for the presidency, Henry was none too impressed. It was a delicate matter, because Henry had been the backbone of the club as president for 25 years and some thought it was like treason to suggest an end to his reign."

(Others didn't, including some guests. Dunn recalled bumping into prominent owner David Moodie in the gents after one of Harrison's protracted Caulfield Cup eve luncheon speeches and the future chairman of Racing Victoria quipped that he could listen to Harrison all day: "In fact, I think I just did!" he said.)

"But we charged John with the responsibility to convince Henry of the need of a succession plan. He did so and Henry's only condition was that John succeeded him. That happened in 1999 and Henry became Patron-In-Chief and John the president, with a succession plan set in stone.

"The other occasion I recall was when a group of us decided to extend our friendships from the Thoroughbred Club with a weekly luncheon at the South Yarra Tennis Club. Henry heard about it and was convinced there was a breakaway group forming, given the group consisted of blokes like Mike Kostos, Des Rowe, Noel McMahon, Tony Ongarello, Fred Bayne, Cameron Fisher, John and me and others.

"Henry was getting really concerned so we assigned John the task of assuring Henry that rather than being a breakaway group, it was in fact fostering the club's ideals. Again, John sorted it all out with his usual diplomacy," Dunn said.

Dillon's connection to the Thoroughbred Club goes back to the days when he attended luncheons at the Hotel Australia.

"I joined the Victoria Amateur Turf Club (now MRC) in 1970, while also acting as (legal counsel) for Sandown greyhounds. My father and Henry Harrison were great mates and I fitted in on both fronts as a son of one and a legal adviser to the other's sporting organisation.

"I was a regular at luncheons before I became a member of the

Thoroughbred Club in March of 1982.

"I then became a VATC committeeman in 1988 and vice-chairman in 1992. When I became president of the Thoroughbred Club for 1999 and 2000, I was happy to be deeply involved in both the club and the race club. And that continued between 2002 and 2005 when I served a three-year term as chairman of the MRC. It was a unique position twice over," he said. Dillon, incidentally, also was president of the Victoria Amateur Football Association.

Another MRC former chairman, Peter Young, speaks effusively about Dillon. "The club is indebted to John, who is a man of integrity and led by example," he said. "John will always be around the Club as racing is in his blood."

Dillion gave the eulogy at the funeral of Henry Harrison and remembers him as an entertaining but forceful character.

"Henry loved to entertain the luncheons by introducing people, in much the same way Ian Wilson did as president of the Carbine Club and as president of the Richmond Football Club.

"At times he went on and on, pointing out a guest or two at one table and then moving from table to table. It seemed at times he was about to acknowledge every person in the room!

"He simply knew so many people and wanted everyone to feel special.

"But Henry was no shrinking violet. He repeatedly rubbished Tom Reynolds, the Sports Minister of the day, because he believed he could do more for the racing industry. It didn't matter to Henry that he was doing it in front of many hundreds at a luncheon. In fact, that inspired him!"

Dillion remains one of the most passionate members of the Thoroughbred Club. He has made an exceptional contribution both as a committeeman/ chairman of the Melbourne Racing Club and as president and prominent Thoroughbred Club member.

However, not even he could bend the rules, as Dunn recalls.

"We were at the Caulfield races one day and hadn't caught up until the last race. So, John said we had best get an ale in the members bar, where he ordered two beers. The man behind the counter said the bar was closed and John stood on his digs and asked if the barman knew who he was. "The bloke replied: 'yes, I know who you are, sir, but the bar is still closed.'"

"John didn't hesitate. He grabbed my arm and said let's get to the committee room for that drink!"

"John has a great sense of humour, he loves a drink and he is a fair-dinkum punter. He got all that from his father and he is as Irish as Irish can be. I know that he and his mate Jim Keogh would regularly have lunch. But they skipped out of town lest they be seen, and always headed to Romeo's restaurant in Toorak where they would eat and drink and tell jokes all afternoon.

"John has been a most loyal and influential member of the Thoroughbred Club from the day he walked in the door," Dunn said.

CRAIG DUNN, a Thoroughbred Club member for 25 years, has known John Dillon most of his life.

"John's father and my business partner (and club stalwart) Jim Broderick were great mates and John and I almost always went to the races with them.

"Jim nominated me for club membership, John seconded me, and, as was the case in those days, Mike Kostos and Des Rowe were my references.

"They were great days and I'm ever so grateful that I ended up in Melbourne and that I became such a close friend of John Dillon. It all started by accident. I was representing KPMG in Melbourne and when my term was up the office in my native New Zealand told me that times were bad. I told them I couldn't wait for the good times to return, so I wasn't returning.

"So, here I was in Melbourne, an accountant looking for work, and a bloke who had owned horses since I was in my early 20s. I hooked up with Jim Broderick, who introduced me to his mate Sir John Dillon and his son John and away we went.

"I've owned plenty of horses, but the best was Cunamulla Lass, who won the Listed Strutt Stakes in Hobart, was runner-up in the Listed 1000 Guineas in Hobart and was third in the Listed Launceston Oaks.

"The best time is being part of the Thoroughbred Club. It is the best group I have been involved with in my life. The whole intention of the group is to have fun. It is not about people championing a cause or pushing their own barrow. It is about people getting together to have fun as well as being involved in something everyone loves, racing. This club has real spirit and that's what makes it great," Dunn said.

"This club has real spirit and that's what makes it great"

ROGER JENNINGS has earned the reputation of being unflappable, efficient and dedicated, but even he can remember the day in June of 2015 when he almost threw himself off the train in despair.

Jennings, who stepped in as secretary of the Thoroughbred Club when Ian Scroggie travelled to Scotland 14 years ago and has held the post since, was happily travelling to Caulfield when he had a phone call from the offices of the Melbourne Racing Club. In a nutshell, the official wanted to know why 50 people were gathered outside the Trustees room, because the MRC had a special meeting there that day.

"When I explained we had our monthly meeting there that day, with Mark Read our guest speaker, the official politely replied: 'No, your luncheon is scheduled for tomorrow!'

"I could have died on the spot. He was right. As unusual as it was, we had organised the luncheon for the Wednesday, not the usual Tuesday, but I had sent out a letter giving the wrong day and was even convinced myself that it was on the Tuesday.

"Anyway, the MRC did us proud and put an end to my embarrassment by organising the back room at the Glasshouse (in the Tabaret) and the luncheon went off without a hitch. I'm not sure how many people knew of the stuff-up, but it all worked out in the end," Jennings said.

After 14 years in the hot-seat, it was a mistake so rare that none of the presidents he has helped — Geoff Dawson, Gary Lechte, John Connellan and Cameron Fisher — can recall another.

Jennings is charged with the responsibility of being all things to the club, with countless chores hidden behind the obvious challenges of organising the Blue Diamond Stakes eve and Caulfield Cup eve gala luncheons.

"In the early days we sent everything out by mail, writing up invoices on a typewriter for members' subs as well as notices of up-coming monthly meetings and the big events, putting them in envelopes and licking a lot of stamps before posting them.

"We had only 60 members in those days but now we have 183. And we sent out quarterly accounts whereas we do them annually these days.

"Fortunately, my wife Nerryll became computer literate well before me and she was an amazing help.

"These days it is easier on computers, but you still must send out notices, do the accounts, organise guest speakers and the venues, sought out the numbers and seating arrangements, organise stud tours and the like. It never really ends," he said.

"And one of the most important tasks is to seek out sponsors because, although we are on solid financial ground, everything is so expensive these days. The members' fees, sponsorship money from the Thoroughbred Club race day and profits from our major luncheons only just covers our expenses.

"But the club made the decision some time ago that we are not about building assets, we are about having fun events. The gala 50th anniversary dinner is an example — it cost a pretty penny but for everyone who attended, it was worth every cent.

> "Henry Harrison was the boss and whatever he said was gospel"

"The same goes for all our activities. Geoff Dawson, Gary Lechte, John Connellan and now Cameron Fisher are presidents who push that line. They have different personalities, but the common denominator with them all is that the happiness of the members is paramount.

"I've been lucky to have been secretary under those four gentlemen. When Ian Scroggie was secretary, Henry Harrison was the boss and whatever he said was gospel. In my time, we have much more debate with an excellent but stable committee all expressing their opinions, making it a more democratic process," he said.

Jennings, joined the club in June 1991 after eight years as a guest of Bill Kollosche. "I was an insurance broker and Bill owned Ferntree Gully and Lilydale Mitsubishi and we became good friends. He put me up as a member, and Bill Vass seconded me.

"Bill won the club's owner's award in 1992 and owned a lot of horses, and I actually leased my first horse from him, a nag named Raging River who was trained by Jim Kennedy. She won three city races and was runner-up in the Thousand Guineas, but it was pretty much downhill after that.

"I guess I've been lucky because I've had 23 city wins. Besides Raging River, some of my winners included Sober Star who won five races including the $50,000 Kyneton Guineas; Atvino who cost $200,000, Staanray who won two in a row in town; Gumboot who did the same and my last winner was Galloping Hill.

"I bred her granddam, dam and her and she won three races, one at Sandown and a second placing at Flemington. Unfortunately, she couldn't get in foal," Jennings said.

Jennings decided to get into breeding and at one stage had 23 mares and foals. However, when he retired from his job, he also retired from the breeding caper. Former president John Connellan is happy about that as he describes Jennings as the lynchpin of the club, stating "the club would collapse without his dedicated work."

"I know in my time as president I would ring Roger almost daily and, especially around the big luncheons, he was intense. People would ring on the eve of the function and say that a couple of guests had pulled out and someone else would ring and say they wanted another two guests on their table.

"He and his wife Nerryll had already organised all the tables and seating arrangements and yet despite the last-minute challenges they handled everything with aplomb. I think his release valve was to move the re-jigged table further down the room as a form of punishment."

Connellan said the only time he saw Jennings crack up with laughter in the face of an impending disaster was the year when he organised the Australian Youth Choir to perform at the start of the Caulfield Cup eve luncheon.

"The first year I organised an opera singer to perform *This is the moment* as Ron Hutchinson walked into the room carrying the Caulfield Cup. It was stirring stuff.

"But the next year I organised the Australian Youth Choir to perform the national anthem. I was standing on stage a few minutes before the scheduled start and suddenly realised what I had done. I burst out laughing and Roger came over to ask what was up. I told him and then Gary Lechte saw both of us buckled over and he came up too.

"As I explained, what do you think everyone will do once the choir starts singing the national anthem? Stand, of course. And how do you think they will see Ron Hutchinson when 800 people are standing?

"Of course, it was the disaster I figured. Ron could have carried the Caulfield Cup on his head and still nobody would have noticed him walking into the room!

"When I look back, it was the only time Roger had tears of laughter when something clearly was going to go wrong. Mostly he is seriously anxious that nothing goes amiss. He sets exceptionally high standards for himself to ensure the members and guests enjoy every minute of our functions," Connellan said.

PETER DEVITT carries a card in his wallet that makes a mockery of credit cards.

On the card is a list of racehorses currently running for him, all trained by David Hayes. At a club luncheon in May 2018, he had 43 names on the card!

That didn't include the names of 18 broodmares he owns, or the most important investment he has in his racing stable — the stallion Nicconi.

"I own 40 per cent of Nicconi and he pays for all my gallopers (expenses) these days," Devitt said.

Devitt and his late mate Les Gordon began on a high when the first galloper they went into — King's High — won the Victoria Derby in 1988.

"A year later he won the Australian Guineas and we were both hooked. In fact, when VOBIS first started that year we were involved in the most horses by any owners — more than 30 as I recall.

"It has been great fun, from our time with Colin, then David and Peter and Tony McEvoy in between before David returned from Hong Kong. We have been with Lindsay Park from the get-go and enjoyed multiple Group 1 winners.

"It all started when we approached Colin to race a horse with him and he said that racing was a numbers game and that we should get five blokes to buy five horses and expand our chances of success. So, Robert Sangster, former South Australian football champion Ken Eustice, broker Chris Payne and Les and I kicked it off. Our colours went on King's High and we were off and running.

"King's High was our first Group 1 winner, but then we had to wait about 20 years before Niconero came along. He won the Futurity Stakes twice (2008 and '09), the Kingstown Town Stakes (2008) and the Fruit 'n' Veg (2006) and the 2009 Australian Cup, which pretty much made up for the barren years.

"Nicconi followed and he won the Lightning Stakes (2010) and The Galaxy (2009) before North Boy won the Krisflyer in Singapore and Confectioner was runner-up in the Ranvet Stakes in Sydney.

"Nicconi proved a sensation for us. I owned 50 per cent, David Hayes 25 per cent and Les Gordon 25 per cent when he raced. We sold 30 per cent of the stallion to Widden Stud when he retired (10 per cent off each owner's share) and so I ended up with 40 per cent of him at stud."

At $24,750 per service fee in 2018, that's big money given, according to Devitt, "he has served more than 200 mares for each of the past two seasons."

"So, he is currently paying for all my other horses. All he needs to do is produce a Group 1 winner and then, well..."

GRAEME SAMPIERI has been instrumental in "the production line" of the Thoroughbred Club, having nominated more members to the club than he can remember.

"After I joined in November of 1979, I had three tables at the Thoroughbred Club luncheons. I reckon I initiated a lot of people to become members from those luncheons, people such as John Connellan and Peter Devitt and the like."

Sampieri was the second bookmaker to join the club, following Mark Read. Along the journey he has rubbed shoulders, if not taken a bet from, hundreds of club members and their guests.

His flamboyant career began officially in 1966 when, on the advice of John H. Griffiths, he took out a licence. However, he had long been involved in the caper. Ever since he was old enough to work in his father's Kew fruit shop he knew about betting — his father paid out the local SP bookie every Friday afternoon.

The eldest of four brothers was raised in the back room of his parents' fruit shop but was sent to Ballarat to board and be educated by the nuns between the ages of six and 14. He then transferred to St. Pat's Ballarat where he proved to be one of the best sprinters at the school during his time under the Christian Brothers.

"I suppose I had a good chance of making something out of athletics and I played football for Hawthorn firstly in the under 19s and then I was part of the club's first reserves premiership in 1958," Sampieri said.

"But I was just into too much at the same time. Besides helping dad at the fruit shop and the market, playing footy for Hawthorn and running well enough to consider going professional, in 1956 I started a pharmacy course in Swanston Street in the city. "It was all too much and after three years at pharmacy college I gave it away. My uncle lived next door to John Griffiths and worked as a bookie's dog, running all over the betting ring to get odds and back horses.

"I then became manager of his massive doubles odds (remember the early Caulfield-Melbourne Cup double charts!) and eventually he pushed me into taking out my own licence in 1966.

"I saw the best times," Sampieri said. "The bookies then were one of the most powerful and influential group of bookmakers of the last century. They were loud, colourful and were laying odds to a new and robust Australia. The Second World War had ended, and the nation enjoyed full employment. A steady stream of migrants from across the world arrived on our shores, first willing to work hard but play just as hard.

> "It is sad to see what has happened to bookmakers now. In our heyday it was all about cash and bookies were fearless,offering the best odds and never flinching when it came to big bets"

"It is sad to see what has happened to bookmakers now. In our heyday it was all about cash and bookies were fearless, offering the best odds and never flinching when it came to big bets," the now octogenarian said.

"John H. Griffiths was a remarkable bookmaker. He wouldn't flinch when taking a big bet, he knew everything that was going on. He was so powerful that everyone who wanted a commission placed on a race would come to John H. No wonder they called him the Godfather."

Sampieri wrote bets for prime ministers, premiers, High Court judges and, as he said, "the odd bank robber" who was trying to wash some cash from a hold-up three days earlier.

"They were amazing times. I remember the late Bill Collins, a great race caller and a very smart punter, regularly having $10,000 to win $1000 the place on a horse or greyhound. Bill had a share in a bookmaking business. He was the son of a country bookie in East Gippsland and, as Sampieri explained, the system in those days allowed for a substitute whereby a person could be nominated to stand up for another (the bankroller).

"That left time for Bill to do all his radio and TV commitments. He was a huge, and I mean huge, place better. He would talk short odds, but he was such a good form analyst that he invariable won."

Sampieri became known as "St. Graeme" for his generosity. His many acts of charity were known only to those close to him. He admits that it broke his heart to see colleagues he had stood next to for decades drop out of the game and, in his words, "end up without a stamp".

Those who know Sampieri intimately maintain nobody ever went without a meal when the bookie was aware of their circumstances. But there were times when Sampieri reckons he wondered where his next meal would come from after tough days at the track.

"The worst day of my life," he recalls, "was the 1976 Melbourne Cup won by Van Der Hum. There was no real threat of rain on Cup day but when he arrived at Flemington the track was hit with a deluge of rain, and from the outset the punters wanted nothing but the New Zealander. They back him from 10/1 into 8/1 into 5/1 to the exclusion of all others. I thought he much have been a duck.

"It was so wet that I couldn't get off my stand to bet back so I was caught with the lot. Van Der Hum won, and I'd done a stack, more than any time prior or since.

"Then I finally jumped off the stand and sought out some of the drier ground in the betting ring. It was then that Jack Taylor, a regular punter with me, came over and asked if he could get $2000 each way on a runner in the last at Morphettville.

"It was at double-figure odds but after such a disastrous day I thought to myself that this bloke never wins, so I hold the bet. It wins by about eight lengths and another $20,000+ jumps out of the bag."

Sampieri also tells the story of a client who rang him in the mid-1970s on Oaks night during the carnival. The punter wanted to have coffee the next morning and needed a favour.

"We met in Toorak Road at a restaurant and he gave me all of these cheques that he wanted me to pass on to bookmakers on the final day of the carnival for his settling. But after the conversation went on I said: 'you've got a horse running in the big race on Saturday. Why aren't you backing it?' and he says, 'No, I don't think it's got any hope'. And I said: 'What's the trainer think?' and he replies: 'It's got a strong each-way chance but look, it's 33/1. It can't win.'"

Sampieri said: "Look, just for the hell of it, I will have $2000 each way on it for you just in case."

Sampieri put $1000 each-way on the horse at 40/1 with another bookie and put the extra $1000 each-way through his own book.

The punter's horse came down the outside and won in a photo. "While I was just coming to terms with what happened, out of the crowd comes my friend wanting to have me knighted."

"There were the days when leviathan punter Kerry Packer would have bookies trembling during the spring carnival"

Then there were the days when leviathan punter Kerry Packer would have bookies trembling during the spring carnival.

"He bet with me half-a-dozen times. He was very dangerous because he would bet in hundreds of thousands. Worse, he would ring with a minute before jump and want $100,000 or more on a runner and just hang up, leaving you no time to say no if that's the way you wanted it. I actually got him for a lot of money over one carnival, and perhaps that's why he looked elsewhere, leaving me alone."

For Sampieri, those days now form part of his fond memories of half-a-century as a bookmaker. His son Mark, who worked alongside him for 15 years until 2001 when he took out his own bookmaking licence and with his father in 2003 opened the first Victorian corporate bookmaking partnership, now is carrying on the famous Sampieri legacy.

JOHN RUSSELL was front and centre from the beginning of The Thoroughbred Club and remembers those days for the fun and frivolity that helped link a variety of people with the common love of horse racing.

"I gave the first phantom call of the Caulfield Cup at the inaugural function in October of 1968 and the following month Supreme Court Judge Arch Fraser and I were made Honorary Members. I was made an Honorary Life Member in 2000," he recalls.

"I did phantom calls from 1968 until 2003, when Ted Ryan took over, and I had a fair bit of success with the calls.

"I remember my first call in '68 when I was sitting at a table at The Hotel Australia with Glenn Stott, who owned Bunratty Castle. He declared to me that it would win the Caulfield Cup by four lengths, even though it was a 12/1 shot. He was flamboyant: a man who imported watches and who wasn't backwards with his opinions.

At the table also were Sir Reg Ansett who owned Impellar in the race and Philip Ismael who owned Always There.

"When it came to the call, I went with Stotty to win, and you wouldn't believe it the horse won as easily as he'd predicted. That made me look pretty good and everything rolled from that.

"Naturally I was invited back and over the years I did phantom calls at the Hotel Australia, the Southern Cross and Leonda. And you had to be on your toes because the smarties would clock your call and have a go if it was too slow!

"What I remember about those days was that after the luncheon at the Hotel Australia we would adjourn to the bar where we inevitably stayed too late, even though the next day was a big occasion with the running of the Caulfield Cup.

"Fortunately for me, Bert Bryant was doing the race calling then and my task was simply doing interviews. There was no way I could have stuck on drinking after the Thoroughbred Club luncheon like I did and then front to accurately call the Caulfield Cup the next day! They were big sips that went long into the night.

"However, chatting to a few people during the following day made it easy for me to give my all at both events."

Russell, 83, retired in 2003 after calling for 30 years with 3UZ and 15 years with Sky Channel. He said the Thoroughbred Club has helped promote horse racing and enabled so many people of different backgrounds to bond socially.

"It has been a marvellous, popular club for half a century. When it began, we had a judge, a watch importer, a baker, a politician, a doctor, a media man, club committeemen, secretaries and almost every profession under the sun.

"New chums today are having just as much fun as we did 50 years ago"

"There were only two dozen of us then and now there are close to 200 yet the cosmopolitan look of the club remains. And the new chums today are having just as much fun as we did 50 years ago."

Russell recounts the tale of an owner who looked at his bill one day and saw he was being charged for Sunday syrup.

Intrigued, the Club member contacted the prominent trainer and queried the bill.

"That's for when you come to the stables, pat your horse and have a beer with me — that's Sunday syrup," he said.

PETER LAWRENCE has been one of the most amiable and enthusiastic members of the Thoroughbred Club, enjoying Honorary Membership for 12 years while chairman of the Victoria Amateur Turf Club (Melbourne Racing Club) before taking out membership at the end of his chairmanship in 2000.

Lawrence, who remained on the MRC committee until retiring in 2009, was honoured in 2011 for his decades of service when the J. J. Liston Stakes was renamed the P. B. Lawrence Stakes, a Group 2 weight-for-age feature over 1400m run at the start of the spring carnival.

To boot, the club named the Skyline Level 3 dining/entertainment area of the Rupert Clarke Grandstand the Peter Lawrence Room.

Lawrence was instrumental in orchestrating the funding for the grandstand, as he was for initiating the annual Back To Caulfield race day which pays tribute to returned service people.

Lawrence raced many gallopers with Bruce Elkington and loved to socialise with owners, breeders and trainers. He was the guest speaker at the Thoroughbred Club and toasted the Caulfield Cup at the race eve luncheon as well as presenting winners' trophies.

He was an Honorary Member of the Thoroughbred Club throughout his chairmanship of the Victoria Amateur Turf Club until his 12-year reign ended in 2000 and he then became a member.

"The race must have been 'rigged' for the Queen to have backed a 33/1 winner"

One of the most entertaining stories about Lawrence comes from Alan Green, who before winning Melbourne Cups with Almandin and Rekindling, raced the top galloper Venus And Mars.

"It was the Spring of 1981, and Venus and Mars had won his maiden at Geelong. His next start was at Caulfield on a special day's racing put on for Her Majesty The Queen.

"We were running in the Westminster Handicap for three-year-olds and Queen Elizabeth was there which made it very exciting.

"Peter was President of the VATC then, and he tipped Venus And Mars to the Queen's protocol officer.

"Well, Venus And Mars won easily and the following day, on page three of Wednesday's *Sun* newspaper, over two-thirds of the page was an article on how the Queen had backed him at 33/1.

"That led to publicity later in the week that the race must have been 'rigged' for the Queen to have backed a 33/1 winner. Peter thought it was hysterical but had to keep a straight face in his role as club president," Green recalled.

ADAM SANGSTER, the Thoroughbred Club vice-president for the 50th year celebrations, only too vividly remembers his foray into the racehorse fold.

"It was 1984 when I was 18, just out of Harrow boarding school — you know, a place where you are dropped off at the age of seven and picked up at the age of 18.

"I was sent to Cambridge Stud for a season, during my gap year. Dad (Robert) had 15 breeding rights to Sir Tristram and all the mares were housed at Sir Patrick Hogan's New Zealand property.

"I recall later in the season, around 2am on November 4, I helped foal down Marauding, and two hours later Kapstaad out of "blue hen" mare Eight Carat. When Kaapstad popped out, beautifully black with four white socks, one of Sir Patrick's lads and my roommate during my trip, Shane Keating, suggested I lease it off my father.

"So, to clinch the deal I gave 10 per cent to dad's racing manager, 40 per cent to Keating and kept the other 50 per cent myself.

"I then went to legendary trainer Terrance Millard in South Africa for a term and decided to call the horse Kaapstad, which is Afrikaan for Cape Town, which I spelt wrong.

"Then I went back to England and worked in a merchant bank, during which time Kaapstad won an important lead-up race to the Golden Slipper.

"Dad shouted me tickets to fly to Sydney for the race — I remember watching *Crocodile Dundee* in flight — and arriving at the renowned Sebel Town House Hotel where, bold as brass at the age of 21, I proceeded to drink with the big boys of racing.

"We set a record bar bill of $15,000 (they put a plaque on the wall to commemorate it), including $350 of Sambuca shots after dad and his senior contingent had left.

"The last thing I remember is being carried, shit-faced, to my room at 4am. On the way we passed our trainer, Colin Hayes OAM, who was heading to trackwork. I will never forget the look on his face as he saw me lurching towards the lift.

"A few hours later dad woke me, took one look at me and told me I was in no condition to go to the races. I didn't, couldn't, put up a fight so I grabbed a glass of orange juice, threw it up everywhere, and have never had an orange juice since.

"Dad was talking about the horses — he had four in the Golden Slipper — and going on and on and I seriously didn't take in a word of it. I passed out again and woke to the television news which was replaying the race. I couldn't make out any of dad's famous green and blue colours, so I figured it was not our day. Then I saw my step-mother, Sue, leading in Marauding.

"I roused myself and headed downstairs dressed in my bag of fruit only to discover that dad and his team had been taken by members of the Sydney Turf Club committee and others to a celebratory dinner. Then one of the leading journalists in the bar asked me about Kaapstad. I mumbled something like it just wasn't his day and was completely embarrassed when informed that he didn't run and he had been sold that morning before the Slipper.

"I had agreed to the sale earlier that morning but had no memory of it"

"Obviously I had agreed to the sale earlier that morning but had no memory of it. Anyway, it was a good day all round: dad won the Golden Slipper with Marauding and also had sold Kaapstad to a New Zealand stud for a then Southern Hemisphere record price, and I enjoyed the windfall of funds until I gave a significant part of it back in the October '87 stock market crash," Sangster said.

Kaapstad had royal blood, being by Sir Tristram out of a mare from the great Eight Carat family. Before he went to stud, the half-brother to Octagonal won seven races for Colin Hayes, including the Group 1 VRC Sires' Produce Stakes and the Group 2 Ascot Vale Stakes.

"He produced seven Group 1 winners among 43 stakes winners and I will always remember him from his birth and the considerable money I collected for his sale," Sangster said.

Sangster, who believes his other best horses were champion sprinter Isca and Victoria Derby winner Blackfriars, is the owner of Swettenham Stud and son of legendary racehorse owner and breeder Robert Sangster. After stints in finance in England and Hong Kong, Sangster arrived in Australia in 1991 and was actively involved in the day-to-day operations of Collingrove Stud which was a joint venture between the Sangster and Hayes families.

Several years later Adam oversaw Collingrove Stud shift the centre of its operation from the Hunter Valley in New South Wales into Nagambie in the North-East region of Victoria with star sire Rory's Jester making the trip south, with Bluebird, Scenic and Danehill Dancer.

Adam became a managing partner of Collingrove in 1996 and later that year was responsible for introducing breeding giants Darley to the Australian market, at their property in the Hunter in 2000.

In 2004, he became a naturalised Australian and the following year ended the Sangster-Hayes joint venture by buying out both family interests and rebranding Collingrove Stud as Swettenham Stud. Four years later the farm presented for sale the daughter of Bel Esprit and Helsinge. She was Black Caviar, the world champion sprinter who was unbeaten in 25 career runs.

Sangster then became a director of both the Thoroughbred Breeders Of Australia and national thoroughbred marketing and promotions company Aushorse. He said the Thoroughbred Club, which Robert attended whenever he was in town, was a union of like-minded racing people who wanted the industry to flourish, and for the good times to be enjoyed by all. The Sangster family, of course, has had much to do with both sides of that mission.

The late Robert Sangster was a revolutionary and famed owner/breeder, having left an indelible mark on the international thoroughbred industry. The winners of 210 Group 1 races worldwide in 22 counties have raced in the famous colours or were bred and sold by the farm. Legendary names that come to mind include Lomond, The Minstrel, El Gran Senor, Detroit, Belldale Ball, Marauding, Special, Alleged, Storm Bird and, of course, one of history's greatest sires, Sadler's Wells.

A successful business man, Robert's legendary buying raids at the Keeneland yearling sales turned the industry on its head and he was a pioneer of the shuttle stallion. And he, like Adam, enjoyed living the good life.

WARREN BROWN, a vice-president in the year of the 50th anniversary of the Thoroughbred Club, has celebrated his connection with the club in many different capacities since 1991 — more likely than not with a beer in hand.

To be fair, that was a requirement for the first decade when he was supplying the beer and wine for the club's lavish luncheons.

"I was involved initially when CUB (of which he was the boss) began sponsoring the Caulfield Cup in 1991," he recalled.

After a distinguished 20-year career at Elders IXL and Carlton & United Beverages from 1982 to 2002, Brown joined the Melbourne Racing Club committee and became a Thoroughbred Club member in 2002.

He then took over as chief-executive of the MRC in 2004 and has continued his involvement since.

Brown won the Thoroughbred Club owners award in 2010 and he had double reason to celebrate.

"I won mainly because of the feats of Above Average, who was part of the Lee Freedman-operated Ball & Chain syndicate. He was third in the Bart Cummings, second in the Moonee Valley Cup, Sandown Cup and Manion Cup. I was a bit embarrassed to win but Above Average gave me enough points in a low-scoring year to snare it.

"At that stage I was the chief executive of the Melbourne Racing Club as well as being a club member, so it was nice to be so heavily involved when I won the trophy," he said.

Brown has been an invaluable contributor, utilising his mix of experience, business expertise, racing knowledge and his renowned marketing acumen and strong leadership and planning skills.

And his social habits!

THE THOROUGHBRED CLUB OWNERS AWARD began in the 1969/70 season as an "in-house" winning owners competition.

In the early years, only a few members had any chance of winning because an owner could nominate all the horses he owned, and it didn't matter if he were only a part-owner, so long as his name was in the race book. And the competition involved all races, both city and country.

Various qualifying requirements followed almost annually to provide as equal a playing field as possible.

"But it was tough," explained Ian Scroggie. "A system was introduced whereby the points were double for a city win over a country win, but that didn't help much because the 'big boys' ran horses everywhere.

"To say winning this competition was taken extremely seriously by the members is an understatement"

"Then there was the case of Mark Read who won in 1981 with his massive collection of super gallopers. His stable of stars looked like winning for years to come so an executive decision was made that he would in future be ineligible — rules were installed that only locals could enter, and Mark was living in Sydney.

"To say winning this competition was taken extremely seriously by the members is an understatement.

"For the record, David Hains won the competition in 1982 and 1983 with 149 points and 102 points respectively. I happened to collate and record Mark's votes for those years and they were 215 and 301.5 respectively! Mark took his ineligibility in the spirit intended, which was great because he simply would have been a standout every year with his gallopers.

"Then there was a system where a member was awarded 8 points if he was the individual owner of a winner, four points if he and a partner owned it, and two points if a syndicate of more than two owned it.

"That came about because of the seemingly unbreakable streak of Merv

Brown, who won it five seasons in a row.

"He owned more than 100 gallopers, and to make sure he gleaned full points for every win, he changed the ownership papers so that his wife was no longer a partner! As I said, it was serious business. Merv Brown was a true racing man, the owner of Hang Ten clothing who sponsored the Blue Diamond for five years until he fell on hard times.

"He changed the ownership papers so that his wife was no longer a partner!"

"Finally, in the 1987/1988 racing season, Brown's stranglehold was broken. The committee changed the rules so that a member could nominate only four horses at the start of the season and could include a substitute only if one of the original nominations was injured or retired, and not because he wasn't successful.

"That lead to a fair go for everyone, and the competition remains one of the most hotly contested and keenly sought trophies.

"Our late member Keith Southwick will always be remembered for his generosity in providing the Gold Cup Club perpetual trophy for three decades and providing a small replica Gold Cup for every winner of the competition.

"He presented the trophy every year and came close to winning it himself, finishing runner-up four times. But he was in good company, because Henry Harrison never won it either," Scroggie said.

THE HENRY HARRISON THOROUGHBRED CLUB LEADING OWNER TROPHY WINNERS

1970 D.S. Dabscheck
1971 D.S. Dabscheck
1972 T.R. Trevaskis
1973 T.R. Trevaskis
1974 T.R. Trevaskis
1975 W.W. Cockram
1976 W.W. Cockram
1977 M.C. Millson
1978 M.C. Millson
1979 G.A. Bellmaine
1980 G.A. Bellmaine
1981 M.J. Read
1982 D.H. Hains
1983 D.H. Hains
1984 M.T. Brown
1985 M.T. Brown
1986 M.T. Brown
1987 M.T. Brown
1988 M.T. Brown
1989 D.H. Hains
1990 A.R. Millson
1991 J. Hoare
1992 W. Kollosche
1993 J. Racovolis
1994 S.R. Harris
1995 D.J. Lauritz
1996 J. Racovolis
1997 G.R. Lechte
1998 J.B. Munz
1999 F. Biesbroek
2000 K. Taylor
2001 P.B. Lawrence
2002 W.R. Lanyon
2003 R. Menzies
2004 Dr R. Taranto
2005 G.T. Ryan OAM
2006 L.C. Gordon
2007 W.R. Lanyon
2008 P.B. Lawrence
2009 P.B. Devitt
2010 W. Brown
2011 N. Pinder
2012 M. Pilkington
2013 R. Roulston
2014 R. Herron
2015 D. Humphries
2016 R. Gordon
2017 R. Gordon

LES GORDON and son Russell share a unique record at the Thoroughbred Club as the only father/son to each win the owners' award.

Les saluted in 2006 and Russell in 2015 and 2016.

"I never entered the competition while dad was alive. I just loved to see dad and his mate and business partner Peter Devitt battle it out. They had a private battle and loved to out-do each other regardless of the overall result. Peter won it in 2009.

"He and dad would nominate different horses for the competition, even though they were both involve in so many together.

"Then after dad died in 2012, I decided to have a go in 2015 and 2016 and was lucky enough to win, beating Peter Devitt because of one horse, Keen Array.

"The trick to getting points, which are the same for a maiden in the bush as they are in a Group 1 win at Flemington, is to get promising young gallopers. In my first successful year, David Hayes got Keen Array to win a Geelong maiden, a Benchmark 64 at Racing.com Park, an open handicap at Moonee Valley and the Listed Blue Sapphire at Caulfield. He earned a lot of points, while Hear The Chant also won the Thoroughbred Club Stakes during the Caulfield carnival.

"Then last year Keen Array won another two Listed races at Caulfield to give me a kick over Peter, who is not an owner of the horse even though my younger brother Craig (whom Peter nominated for club membership) and Mark Pilkington are. "It is unusual that he is not involved in a galloper trained and part-owned by David Hayes, but that is the quirk of it. Keen Array is one horse I'm sure makes Peter cringe every time he races!

"Peter and dad (Les) were builders together as owners of L. U. Simon Builders and they lucked-in with their first galloper, King's High, who won the 1988 Victoria Derby.

"He got the best of both worlds that day!"

"I remember it so well. It was November 4 and dad went to Flemington to cheer home their horse, which was trained by Colin Hayes.

"After the races and the celebrations, he had to make it to hospital to see his new-born grandson, my son Scot. He got the best of both worlds that day!

"Peter and Les have been with the Hayes family since the mid-1980s, and I have followed. I've had horses trained by Colin, David, the late Peter and Tony McEvoy when he stood in for David when he was in Hong Kong.

"And in the same way, I've followed them into the Thoroughbred Club. I remember coming as a guest when Henry Harrison was making long speeches at a time they were trying to get more youth into the group.

"I remember telling one of the ladies in my office that I was off to the Thoroughbred Club and she figured I would be having a wow of a time, so

I sent her a photo on my phone — it was of a group of old men nodding off during Henry's speech! She never again thought I was skipping out for fun and frivolity, and I never told her how much fun I was having!

"One of the great things about the club is the wonderful people you meet. In the early days I tried to avoid sitting next to Peter and dad and instead get on a table with a variety of different members. When they saw my name tag they would 'Oh, you are Les's son' and away they would go with terrific stories and memories.

"One thing that has always amazed me is that so much hard work, by the secretary (Ian Scroggie and then Roger Jennings) and the president and committee, goes into ensuring a lot of people enjoy themselves.

"I cannot imagine organising 800 people for a function, the menu, costing, seating arrangements, speakers and entertainers.

"And it is not just the big functions. For keen racing people, the opportunity to have a day out at Swettenham Stud or Darley or Lindsay Park is something special."

But perhaps not as special as winning the TBC owners' trophy!

AT the other end of the scale for points won is the late Peter Theodore, a member between 1981 and 1994.

However, he could boast a special place in the Thoroughbred Club's annual award. He managed only one winner for the 1981 season, but it was a beauty!

His galloper Elounda Bay, trained by Bart Cummings, won Australia's premier sprint, the Newmarket Handicap at Flemington. He finished the season with seven points: a win, a second and a third.

THE THOROUGHBRED CLUB STAKES is one of the major tangible contributions by club members to the thoroughbred industry.

From humble beginnings at Werribee in 1968, the race has evolved into the acclaimed 1200m weight-for-age with penalties event at the Caulfield spring carnival.

It was known as the Thoroughbred Club Breeders Stakes when it was run on February 21, 1974, as a 1400m race for three-year-old fillies and four-year-old mares. The race carried a $6000 stake and a $500 trophy and, as a major bonus, the first four placegetters secured stallion services donated by Thoroughbred Club member studs from Arundel, Stockwell, Broonscourt and Calmody.

The race, given Group 3 status in 1979, moved to Caulfield in 1977 and was run over 1400m for three-year-old fillies only.

Club member Ken Cox won that inaugural Caulfield race with Happy Kitten, and the race has been well supported over the years by club members as the race involved an in-house competition. That year the prizemoney was $12,000 with a $1,000 trophy.

Sir Rupert Clarke (Lady's Slipper in 1979), Merv Brown (Why Julie in 1986), Doug Reid (Mammy in 1990), Nick Columb (Imposera in 1987), Adam Sangster/ Swettenham (Camargue in 1999) and Russell Gordon with Hear The Chant in 2016 have been successful in the race, Robert Sangster won it before Adam became a member with Fear Burst in 1983.

The race faced losing group status in the late 1990s as nominations fell away, mainly as the 1400m event on Caulfield Guineas day was running in competition with Caulfield's Thousand Guineas on the Wednesday.

In 2000, the race was saved when reduced to 1200m with a stake increase from $75,000 to $100,000. That attracted a field of 13 sprinting three-year-old fillies and the significant prizemoney increase helped the race's profile and importance. In that 2000 event, club member David Hains narrowly missed when his galloper Queen was beaten by Arrabeea.

The Thoroughbred Club Stakes today carries Group 3 status and prizemoney of $150,000.

THOROUGHBRED CLUB STAKES WINNERS

2017 - Invincible Star
2016 - Hear The Chant
2015 - Serene Majesty
2014 - Earthquake
2013 - Missy Longstocking
2012 - Cavalry Rose
2011 - Platelet
2010 - Solar Charged
2009 - Avenue
2008 - Damselfly
2007 - Gamble Me
2006 - Splashing Out
2005 - Queen Of The Hill
2004 - Emlozza
2003 - Crown Princess
2002 - Innovation Girl
2001 - Patterns
2000 - Arrabeea
1999 - Camargue
1998 - Speedy Kids
1997 - Cornwall Queen
1996 - Flaming Heart
1995 - Vigil
1994 - Verocative
1993 - Cairncross
1992 - Googs Dream
1991 - Cushion
1990 - Mammy
1989 - Lady Of Perfection
1988 - Boardwalk Angel
1987 - Imposera
1986 - Why Julie
1985 - Tonephil
1984 - Delightful Belle
1983 - Fear Burst
1982 - Sovereign Palace
1981 - Voli Dream
1980 - Biscadale
1979 - Lady's Slipper
1978 - Just Landed
1977 - Miss Expensive
1976 - Happy Kitten
1975 - Vamp / Silver Sari #
1974 - Honoured
1973 - # Orinthos / Fulmina
1972 - Make Mine Roses
1971 - # Abinger / Tina's Joy
1970 - Intention
1969 - Via
1968 - Threat

#Run in divisions

NEVILLE GIBSON has enjoyed more success than most with Group 1 success ranging from 1974 to 2012.

It all began when he joined club members Albert Millson and his late brother Monty Millson to win the Group 1 Epsom Handicap with Citaldel, trained by Noel Kelly.

As Gibson recalls bookmakers freely offered $101 before the winner started at $67."Citadel was a rarity as he won over 1200m and 3200m at Flemington. He inflicted the only defeat on the champion Bletchingly when he won the Bobby Lewis." Despite the windfall, Gibson laments what may have been had Frozen Section won the Group 1 Metropolitan.

"Frozen Section was beaten a short half head (by Passetreul) and we had bet on the double. It would have netted us $250,000 which in 1974 was more than a tidy sum!" he recalls.

Gibson had a great relationship with Noel Kelly, who trained 93 winners for him and his co-owners. He and club member George Sturesteps raced Bonded who won six races in a row and 15 all up. Mrs Gallagher was another grand performer, winning 12 races.

In 2003, Gibson, Sturesteps and other club members John Radley, Arthur Heintz, Neil Oates and the late Bob Taranto won the Group 1 Coolmore Classic with Fashions Afield, who earned the honour of Australian Two-year-old Horse of the Year.

In 2009, Gibson enjoyed a special moment when Bel Mer won the Group 1 Robert Sangster Stakes in Adelaide — special because Robert's son Adam currently is vice-president of The Thoroughbred Club. Bel Mer, trained by Mick Price, won $599,575 in prizemoney and was sold at the Inglis Easter Sales in Sydney for $1,050,000.

Gibson and fellow club members enjoyed many other Group and Listed wins, but another special victory was the Group 1 Blue Diamond Stakes of 2012 with Samaready, trained by Mick Price.

TRADITIONALLY the Thoroughbred Club President welcomed guests and proposed the toast to the Caulfield Cup.

However, from 1998, the club decided to invite race-loving identities to toast the Cup.

1998	Gary Gray
1999	Hon Michael Hodgman QC
2000	Hon Sir James Killen KCMG
2001	Graham Duff, TBC member and Chair of Racing Victoria
2002	Simon O'Donnell
2003	Peter Lawrence, member and Chair MRC
2004	Bruce McAvaney
2005	Dr Alan Bell STC
2006	Lee Freedman
2007	Fred Kersley
2008	Sam Kekovich
2009	Greg Radley
2010	Richard Callander
2011	Peter Lawrence
2012	John Rothfield
2013	Henry Plumptre
2014	David Raphael
2015	Drew Morphett
2016	Ross Stevenson
2017	David Hayes

CAULFIELD AND MELBOURNE CUP WINNERS OWNED BY MEMBERS

The club has a rich history of providing winners of both the Caulfield and Melbourne Cup. As of the 50th anniversary in 2018, club members have been involved in 11 Caulfield Cup wins, and six Melbourne Cup successes. Staggeringly, four of the latter have come in the past seven years!

MELBOURNE CUP

1989 TAWRIFFIC — Ed McKeon was an owner of the New Zealand-bred who provided Lee Freedman with his first Melbourne Cup (and the quinella with Super Impose) and victory for jockey Shane Dye. He won in the then record time of three minutes, 17.1 seconds.

1991 LET'S ELOPE — Dennis Marks celebrated the Cups double in dominant style this year. She won by two-and-a-half lengths from Shiva's Revenge, ahead of Mongolia Hill and Super Impose.

2010 AMERICAIN — Gerry Ryan and Kevin Bamford saluted when the import bolted away for a two and three-quarter length win over Maluckyday, So You Think and Zipping. Trained by Alain De Royer-Dupre and ridden by Gerald Mosse, the stallion now stands at Swettenham Stud, which is owned by club member Adam Sangster.

2013 FIORENTE — Ross Herron celebrated when the Gai Waterhouse-trained stallion, ridden by Damien Oliver, won by three-quarters-of-a-length from Red Cadeaux and Mount Athos.

2016 ALMANDIN — Alan Green enjoyed his first Cup success when the import, trained by Robert Hickmott and ridden by Kerrin McEvoy, fought on doggedly to hold out invader Heartbreak City by a long head with Hartnell third.

2017 REKINDLING — Alan Green could not believe his luck with his second Melbourne Cup in two years, as well as having the race quinella. The three-year-old import, trained by young Joseph O'Brien and ridden by Corey Brown, held out Johannes Vermeer by a long neck.

CAULFIELD CUP

1968 BUNRATTY CASTLE — Glenn Stott's galloper started at 12/1 and won from the front, trained by Kevin Wynne and giving Mick Mallyon the first of three Caulfield Cup wins.

1969 BIG PHILOU — Charlie Gawith celebrated with trainer Bart Cummings when the horse became the first and only horse to win the Caulfield Cup on protest. Roy Higgins protested against Nasouri, ridden by Des Lake, for interference in the home straight. Big Philou was favourite for the Melbourne Cup but was doped and scratched just before the race.

1972 SOBAR — Keith Southwick's star won the race as a three-year-old, beating the ilk of Gunsynd who carried 62kg in a sizzling 2:27.1. However, he tragically broke down when long odds-on favourite in the Victoria Derby.

1974 LEILANI — Owned by Andrew Peacock, she won the AJC Oaks and returned to win the Caulfield Cup before starting favourite and finishing second in the Melbourne Cup.

1978 TAKSAN — Owned by club members Merv Brown and Monty Millson, as well as Albert Millson who joined the club in 1986, this win was one of the closest in a controversial photo finish.

1985 TRISTARC — Owned by Nick Columb and George Smorgon, the four-year-old mare started the 5/1 equal favourite and defeated the other equal favourite, Our Sophia from New Zealand, by a head. She won six Group 1 races and when she retired she held the Australasian prizemoney record for a mare.

1988 IMPOSERA — Nick Columb-owned and Ross McDonald-trained, the mare defeated Congressman in a driving finish with Brian York in the saddle.

1989 COLE DIESEL — Greg Mance was training on the Gold Coast when 8/1 chance Cole Diesel stormed home to win the Cup from the favourite Nayrizi and The Phantom. Mance was not a Thoroughbred Club member at the time but was a frequent attendee. When he returned to Victoria because of ill health, he quickly took up membership.

1991 LET'S ELOPE — Dennis Marks, along with Kevin White, bought the giant chestnut mare and gave her to Bart Cummings. Steven King rode her to the coveted Caulfield/Melbourne Cup double.

1999 SKY HEIGHTS — A brave winner under Damien Oliver for trainer Colin Alderson, he also was beaten by a whisker in 2001 in this race. He was owned by club member Rupert Legh.

2010 DESCARADO — Recently deceased Ross Herron was a part-owner of this import, who provided Gai Waterhouse with her first success in the race. Chris Munce rode the $17 chance to a length win in Heavy 9 conditions.

THOROUGHBRED CLUB members have been associated with some genuine champions of the turf. Three that stand out are Taj Rossi (Vic Peters), Manikato (Mal Seccull) and Sobar (Keith Southwick).

Taj Rossi, according to the late, great jockey Roy Higgins, was the best middle-distance galloper he rode in his illustrious career.

Owned by Vic Peters, who joined the Thoroughbred Club in March of 1969, Taj Rossi was dominant during the 1973 season, culminating in his elevation to Australian Horse of the Year as a three-year-old.

Trained by Bart Cummings, the son of Matrice won the Cox Plate, Victoria Derby, Sandown Guineas, Ascot Vale Stakes, Carrum Handicap and Moonee Valley Stakes in an unforgettable season.

He ended his career of 21 races with nine wins, a second and four thirds.

A virus that troubled the horse throughout his career forced his retirement at the age of four. He spent two years at stud in America where he had moderate success before returning to Australia. Amongst his stakes winners were Taj Eclipse (VRC Oakes) and Merimbula Bay (Doncaster Handicap).

The horse died in 1986 at the age of 15.

Mal Seccull certainly secured a bargain when he paid $3500 for champion galloper Manikato, who went on to win $1,154,210 before he retired — in 1983.

Seccull, who died in November 2015, was a great racing personality and contributor. He was a committee member of the VATC from 1985 until 2006, vice-chairman from 1991 until 1998 and a raceclub Life Member. He also spent 20 years as a member of the Thoroughbred Club, from June of 1986 until he resigned in 2006, the same time he vacated his post as a MRC committeeman.

The mild-mannered Seccull was the living example of how to buy a galloper you fancy, regardless of price, and end up with a champion.

He told trainer Bon Hoysted to but the son of Newmarket Handicap winner Manihi, and in a quirk of fate, when Bon couldn't get to the sales he ordered his brother Bob to do the bidding. Under Bon, Manikato won the 1978 Blue Diamond-Golden Slipper double before developing into an out-and-out champion while in Bob's care as an older horse.

The versatile galloper succeeded at distances from 1000m to 1800m and also ran second to Dulcify in the 1979 Australian Cup (2000m), earning him the title as the Australian Racehorse of the Year for the 1978-79 season.

He became only the second horse after Kingston Town to surpass $1 million in earnings and finished his career with the phenomenal record of 29 wins, nine seconds and four thirds from 47 starts.

He won 25 stakes races, all of which are now Group 1 events, established track records in three races, and was inducted in the Australian Racing Hall of Fame in 2002.

Manikato died in 1984 and was buried at Moonee Valley, the scene of his two Freeway Stakes wins (now the Manikato Stakes) and five William Reid Stakes triumphs. The tall, heavily topped chestnut gelding won the 1978 Blue Diamond Stakes and Golden Slipper double for Bon, who died soon after the latter success. Bob Hoysted then took over and as a three-year-old Manikato won eight races and was second three times from 12 starts.

He started that season with victory in the Ascot Vale Stakes in record time and three weeks later he defeated older horses in the Marlboro Cup. He then won the Caulfield Guineas, and, after a spell, he won the first of his five victories in the William Reid Stakes in 1979.

He then won the Orr Stakes and then won the first of his four Futurity Stakes, in record time.

After being nabbed by Dulcify in the Australian Cup (2000m) he dropped back 500m and won the George Ryder Stakes by six lengths, again in record time.

After a bleeding attack at the end of his four-year-old season, he won the 1981 William Reid, Futurity Stakes and Orr Stakes as a five-year-old, but then damaged his suspensory tendons.

But he bounced back to win the Queen Elizabeth Cup, run in honour of the Queen's attendance at Caulfield, and equalled the course record of 1:35.7.

As a six-year-old he started 11 times for five wins including the Freeway Stakes, Futurity Stakes, Moir Stakes, William Reid Stakes and Memsie Stakes.

He had 47 starts for 29 wins, 9 seconds and 4 thirds, including five successive William Reid Stakes and four Futurity Stakes, winning 11 Group 1 races in all for $1,154,210.

After contracting a virus, he was humanely euthanised on February 13, 1984. He is buried within sight of some of his greatest wins in "Manikato's Garden" at Moonee Valley.

Keith Southwick, a Victoria Racing Club committeeman for many years, enjoyed an extraordinary 1972 with his amazing galloper Sobar.

Sobar is the only horse to win the Underwood Stakes, Caulfield Guineas and Caulfield Cup in the same year, and his win over Stormy Seas and Gunsynd in the Cup was as emphatic as any three-year-old has achieved in the race.

Trained out of Lord Lodge by Ken Hilton, now the stables of Colin Little, Sobar ran the 2400m in 2:27.1.

Southwick was a member of the Thoroughbred Club from May of 1974 until his death, aged 84, in September of 2011.

He was a member of the family that owned the Cedel Group of Companies, the makers of toothpaste, soap and the like, and is remembered as a flamboyant punter. The story goes that, in a bid to camouflage his wagers, he had an arrangement with bookies whereby he would say $10 on a horse when he wanted $100, and $100 when he wanted $1000 and $1000 when he wanted $10,000.

BILL LANYON and sons Ross and Jamie have enjoyed great success as newspaper proprietors and horse owners and provided a rich legacy to the Thoroughbred Club.

Bill was an outstanding footballer who tried his luck with Carlton in the late 1950s but after only a couple of games in the reserves his father, D. C. Lanyon, told him he needed to make up his mind if he wanted to work for the family business in Mildura or keep playing football.

Fortunately for all concerned, Bill returned home. His father had secured a controlling interest in the Elliott Newspaper Group in 1950, a company which dominated the Mildura, Gisborne and Latrobe Valley regions in Victoria with such titles as the *Sunraysia Daily* and *Latrobe Valley Express*.

Today the group publishes newspapers in Mildura, Swan Hill, Kerang, Cohuna, Castlemaine, Kyneton, Morwell, Traralgon and Sale.

Bill became company secretary in 1960 and the manager of the *Sunraysia Daily* in 1988 on his father's death. He controlled the company until 2005 when elder son Ross, an accountancy graduate, became managing director of the *Sunraysia Daily* and Elliott Newspapers Group secretary, and another son, Jamie, the assistant manager of the *Sunraysia Daily*.

Today Ross and Jamie run the company as directors, continuing the family's newspaper lineage.

"There is the best footballer I've ever seen"

Thoroughbred Club treasurer Fred Bayne recounts the tale of the day Bill upstaged two of the VFL's most prominent footballers.

"Bill Langdon was a great character and was a super footballer for Mildura. One of the funniest moments I saw, on a visit to the Mildura Cup, was Bill and former Richmond champ and popular publican Des Rowe and former champion Melbourne captain Noel McMahon walk into a local pub after the races. A drinker saw them enter the pub and shouted out, "There is the best footballer

I've ever seen". Both Des and Noel puffed out their chests expecting to be the hero, when the bloke chimed in, "Yes, Bill Langdon was a real star.'"

Bill became a Thoroughbred Club member in 1990 and Ross, who was awarded an OAM last year for his services to racing and the country community, and Jamie who is 12 years younger, followed their dad into the Club as members in 2012.

Ross has become one of the leading lights in Victorian racing. He was the chairman of Country Racing Victoria for a decade and from 2017 a board member of Racing Victoria.

Jamie said racing and ink are in the family's blood. Ross and Jamie continue to race gallopers under the family umbrella of Clay Hero Racing. Their grandfather was a part-owner of Clay Hero, trained by Rick Hore-Lacy at Caulfield. He won eight of his 20 career starts (and six placings) and his successes included the 1989 Group 1 Oakleigh Plate followed by second in the Group 1 Newmarket Handicap.

Mango's Lunch won the Listed Labor Day Cup in Adelaide in 1995 after saluting in the Donald and Ararat Cups. Czar Hero won the Golden Topaz at Swan Hill in 1998 and the 2000 Kilmore Cup, while Seltrice won the West Australian Derby in 1980.

Two of their major achievements occurred in jumps features when Awakening Dream won the 2012 Grand Annual Steeplechase at Warrnambool for Patrick Payne and Kirribilli Gold won the Australian Hurdle for Robert Smerdon the following year.

"The family has raced horses with a lot of trainers including Robert Smerdon, Russell Cameron, Rick Hore-Lacy, Patrick Payne and even Richard Jolly in Adelaide. We all love it," he said.

Jamie said one of his fondest memories of the Thoroughbred Club Caulfield Cup eve functions was the way his luck in the sweep always frustrated his father.

"Dad had been in the club for decades and had never drawn a horse in the sweep. Then, when I joined I sat at four different tables in the first four years and we drew a horse every time — and managed a few collects! Dad was just so frustrated that it made us laugh, and everyone who knew the story to laugh along with us.

THE GODBY family is synonymous with racing, particularly around Caulfield, and Martin is the latest connection to the Thoroughbred Club.

His grandfather Frank was a renowned trainer of stayers and conditioned Maikai who was unluckily beaten twice in the Melbourne Cup in 1939 (to Rivette) and 1940 (behind Old Rowley) as well as being runner-up in the 1939 Caulfield Cup.

And his great-great-uncle, Norman, was aboard Lord Cardigan who won the 1903 Melbourne Cup, defeating the great mare Wakeful.

His great uncle, Cecil, won three Caulfield Cups with Purser (50/1 into 15/1 in 1924), Gaine Carrington (1933) and Northwind (1936). He trained the great Heroic, and other big wins included Demetrius and Heroic in the Caulfield Guineas; Peter Jackson, Purser and Ortelle's Star in the Moonee Valley Cup; Spectre and Murray Glen in the Australian Cup; Synagogue in the Epsom Handicap; Heroic in the AJC Derby; Heroic and The Monk in the Ascot Vale Stakes, and Heroic in the AJC Breeders Stakes and Champagne Stakes.

His uncle-in-law Bill won the Stradbroke Handicap in Queensland with Wiggle in 1958 when she was a two-year-old. He later took her to America where she won numerous races and became a broodmare, with one of her sons, Sir Wiggle, being a top sire in the US.

Gordon Godby is another relation. He was involved in Moonee Valley administration for 48 of its first 56 years, starting as an office boy and ending up as office manager.

His grandfather Frank trained from 1912 until 1952 and his father Jack, who rode Sir Roseland to victory in the Port Adelaide Cup in 1931, won the Caulfield Cup with Sir Blink in 1958, and won a fortune in the process.

The stable backed the three-year-old, ridden by 20-year-old apprentice Alan Yeomans, from 14/1 into 6/1, and the funds allowed Jack Godby to buy a house in Booran Road and a theatre in Glen Huntly Road that he converted into squash courts.

He had eight squash courts and he ran jazz dances on Friday nights and rock dances on Saturday nights. It also staged six Victorian table tennis championships.

Sir Blink also was runner-up in the Caulfield Cup the following year.

Jack Godby also is credited with building the first weigh station and he knew when the horse's weight was perfect and the ideal time to back them.

Martin is having a second crack at the Thoroughbred Club.

"I was a regular guest of Gary Lechte for almost 20 years and a member between 2002 and 2004. However, the monthly meetings were on a Tuesday and I was so busy with work at my jeans shop in South Yarra that I could rarely attend. So, I dropped out. But as soon as I retired l joined up again as a member in January this year (2018).

Martin recalls the day some well-laid plans were shattered by a brilliant ride by Brent "Babe" Thomson.

"I owned Bare Fist and we were preparing him for a killing at his third run. We engaged the Babe, who wasn't all that keen to ride him because his form showed he was running a very long way down the track, even when third in the Maribyrnong Plate behind the gun sprinter of the day, Rancher.

> "Babe jumped him straight to the front and he led all the way and saluted — at 100/1!"

"We knew this was only a lead-up race for our main goal, which was the next start. We didn't bother having a bet as the instructions to Babe were not to overtax the horse. Anyway, the Babe jumped him straight to the front and he led all the way and saluted — at 100/1!"

Martin, who has owned about 30 horses and who mainly engages David Hayes to train, won four races at Flemington with Bare Fist, which almost made up for the long shot miscalculation.

AMANDA ELLIOTT became the first — and in 50 years the only — female member (honorary) of the Thoroughbred Club in 2017.

That coincided with her appointment in February that year as the Victoria Racing Club's first female Chairman in its 153-year history.

Amanda was elected to the VRC Committee in 2002, making her the second female committee member ever appointed. She went on to become the first female Vice Chairman in 2011 and has been involved in most areas of the club.

Amanda, who has a B.A. from the University of Melbourne, has extensive experience at the highest levels of administration of sport, business and politics.

She comes from a family with a long history of thoroughbred racing, breeding and administration. Her father, Ian Bayles, was also Vice Chairman of the VRC and a long-standing committeeman of the Club.

In 2018, she received the prestigious Lady of Racing Award from the Victorian Wakeful Club in partnership with Racing Victoria. This award celebrates women who have made an outstanding contribution to the thoroughbred racing and breeding industries.

Although Amanda established new ground when she was appointed an honorary member of the club, she will join a growing female presence at the Thoroughbred Club.

As Ian Scroggie explained, women have resisted the temptation to become an integral part of the male-dominated club but have been involved in many ways over the decades.

"Many females do get along, especially to the Caulfield Cup eve and Blue Diamond Stakes eve functions, and to social functions such as the Christmas parties, dinner parties and other social outings.

"There was a period when there was a specific women's luncheon to coincide with the Cup eve luncheon.

"That came about when Peter Lawrence was chairman of the VATC (MRC) and his wife decided that while he was having a good time with the men, she would gather a group of ladies and put on a similar luncheon in the dining room under the old tote board." Scroggie explained that when the club started, there was a male domination of most sports bodies — white lines at race clubs to separate the men and women! — and that men ran sports clubs and women were happy to allow them to do so.

"Even as opposite gender exclusion was relaxed, females did not show a great interest in being part of the club.

"However, there was a break-through when the connections of Beer Street included a lady to whom the doors were finally thrown open to celebrate and award the previous year's winner at the Caulfield Cup eve luncheon in 1971."

By 1988 the club broke new ground when ABC newsreader Mary Delahunty became the first lady to attend a monthly luncheon as guest speaker.

Delahunty was a news journalist for the ABC and Network Ten from 1975 until 1996 and appeared in news and current affairs programs such as *Four Corners* and *The 7.30 Report*. She won a Gold Logie in 1983 and was the ABC's weeknight presenter between 1986 and 1990.

She was elected to the seat of Northcote in the Victorian Legislative Assembly at a 1998 by-election. She was Minister for Education from 1999-2002 and was the Minister for the Arts from 1999-2006, Minister for Women's Affairs from 2002-2006 and Minister for Planning from 2002-2005. She did not contest her seat at the 2006 state elections.

In the modern era, a significant number of women attend the club's major functions, almost always on a social basis. However, they are major contributors to the industry. Elliott is chairman of the VRC, while regulars include breeding guru Jenny McAlpine, former Inglis promotor and now Melbourne Racing Club Foundation officer Adrienne Sarkozy and the former chief executive of 23-years of the Cranbourne race club, Yvonne Blackwood.

PROGRESS can be slow, even for the movers-and-shakers at the Thoroughbred Club. Take sponsorship. At the 1991 committee meeting, then treasurer Michael Kostos raised the question of sponsorship in a bid to

Henry Harrison was the backbone and most influential member of the Thoroughbred Club, serving as president for 25 of its first 50 years.

The original tie (left) commissioned 50 years ago — TC gold embroidery, gold stripes on a blue background.

Where legends gather: Gary Lechte with Australian Racing Hall of Fame trainers Bart Cummings, Lee Freedman, John Hawkes and David Hayes. John Connellan is at the far right and the diminutive bloke in the centre is Irish comedian Noel V Ginnity at the Thoroughbred Club Caulfield Cup eve luncheon in 2006.

Chief steward Terry Bailey tells the Thoroughbred Club the highs and lows of his career before departing for Singapore.

Thoroughbred Club president Gary Lechte chats with media megastar and Collingwood Football Club president Eddie McGuire at a Thoroughbred Club luncheon at Caulfield.

Barry Humphries, aka Sir Les Patterson, with president Gary Lechte's assistants Tanya Moss and Leigh O'Donnell at the Thoroughbred Club Caulfield Cup eve luncheon in 2005.

Ross Heron drinks to his amazing run of success. He celebrates the 2013 Melbourne Cup win of Fiorente, three years on from his Caulfield Cup success with Descarado, also trained by Gai Waterhouse.

The class of 1996. Club members, with president Henry Harrison front and centre, gather at the Caulfield racecourse. A new member that day was current president Cameron Fisher (fourth from left, back row).

The Thoroughbred Club Stakes has been run each year of the first half-century of the club. It was won in 1991 by Cushion, and at the presentation were (l to r) Des Rowe, Henry Harrison, Geoff Dawson, winning trainer John Hawkes, winning jockey Darren Gauci, Ian Scroggie and VATC (Melbourne Racing Club) committeeman Geoff Belmaine.

The Ford boys: Tim, Peter, Brendan, Frank, John and Richard at a Thoroughbred Club luncheon.

Thoroughbred Club members and guests at the Euroa property of David Hayes, enjoying a social function in September of 2017.

One of the infamous (now deflated) footballs with logos that cost Gary Lechte an instant $1000 fine at the Thoroughbred Club Caulfield Cup eve function.

Veteran Thoroughbred Club member and former champion Fitzroy footballer Tony Ongarello.

Secretary Roger Jennings, The Hon Craig Ondarchie MP, and president Cameron Fisher at Parliament House, the venue of the Horse's Birthday function in 2017.

Mike Kostos has been a stalwart of the Thoroughbred Club, serving on the committee as well as being treasurer between 1994 and 1998 before becoming a Life Member in 2013.

Bloodstock agent Dean Humphries has been a big contributor to the Thoroughbred Club.

Gary Lechte was president for seven years and introduced fun and entertainment as part of the club's mandate.

Prominent horse owner, breeder and businessman Peter Devitt has been an integral member of the Thoroughbred Club.

Tony Clifford and Andre Kassay enjoy some entertainment at the 50th anniversary party at Rippon Lea in 2018.

Former Thoroughbred Club president Gary Lechte always seems to pull a rabbit out of the hat when it comes to entertainment.

John Dillion has played a unique role as the president of the Thoroughbred Club and chairman of the Melbourne Racing Club.

Father Joe Giacobbe gives Tony Cavanagh a lesson on the finer things in life at the 50th anniversary extravaganza at Rippon Lea in 2018.

Adam Sangster and John Connellan enjoy the entertainment at Rippon Lea during the 50th anniversary extravaganza dinner in 2018.

Above: The Thoroughbred Club powerbrokers of 2018 at the 50th anniversary party at Rippon Lea: (l to r) Peter Devitt, John Connellan, Fred Bayne, Cameron Fisher, Adam Sangster, Gary Lechte and Roger Jennings. Absent: Committeemen Warren Brown and Geoff Dawson.

President Cameron Fisher, Rod Nicholson, secretary Roger Jennings and guest speaker, champion trainer Darren Weir in 2018.

cut costs, particularly for the Caulfield Cup eve luncheon. Chairman Henry Harrison acknowledged the rationale behind sponsorship but made the point that the Thoroughbred Club was a "sponsor" of the VATC itself and did not want to lose its identity in any way.

It was agreed that Kostos should investigate limited forms of sponsorship (product usage) and report back.

It took until 2009 — another 18 years — before sponsorship of the club came into vogue when flamboyant bookmaker Alan Eskander's Betstar threw its weight behind the club.

Betstar was the first official sponsor and was replaced by Sportingbet for a time before BetStar returned.

During the 50th anniversary year, major sponsors are Ladbrokes, Treasury Wine Estates, the Melbourne Racing Club, Inglis, Winning Edge, Swettenham Stud and Honan Insurance Group.

ALAN GREEN would never put his house on a horse. However, he did pay off his abode with only the second horse he owned.

And today, after two Melbourne Cup successes in the past two years, he and wife Barb still live on the 10-acre block among the trees at Jan Juc on Victoria's southern coastline along the Great Ocean Road.

Green, the now retired mastermind behind the Quicksilver franchise, has been interested in racing since before his teens.

He recalls being caught out by adult friends of the family when attending Moonee Valley races as an 11-year-old, and more importantly as a 15-year-old plonking his school fees on Midlander at Flemington, only to lose the lot when the galloper ran second.

But it wasn't until the start of the 1980s that Green began to take the plunge into horse ownership.

"Brian Singer, Barb and I bought Venus And Mars from a girlfriend of ours for $10,000 after Meggs Elkington advised us to buy the son of Sobar. He went to Meggs' property Carawatha near Winchelsea and he set him for the Australian Derby in Perth in 1981.

"The race was run on Boxing Day and was sponsored by Channel Seven which wanted the race to have a 30-minute lead-up time to the 6.30pm news in the eastern states.

"Channel Seven wanted this race to attract a big audience, and because there was so much on in other sports on Boxing Day, they increased prizemoney to make it the richest three-year-old race in the Southern Hemisphere.

"Barb and I were building our home back then and we didn't have the money to finish it. So, we were going to go as far as we could, then camp there until we could finish it.

"That was the plan until Venus, ridden by Johnny Miller, won the Derby. We took eight photocopies of the cheque!

"We finished our house and vowed never to mortgage it. And we still live there today."

Brian, Barb and Alan also bred Entisaar and sold it at the yearling sales to champion South African trainer Mike De Kock on behalf of one of the sheiks. She won at Group 1 and Group 2 level and was the champion South African two-year-old of 2015.

"We retained her younger full sister, Purrari, who is trained by Gai Waterhouse," Alan said.

Another success paved the way for Alan to become a member of the Thoroughbred Club.

"Barb and I owned a leg of Samaready, a More Than Ready two-year-old trained by Mick Price who won the 2012 Group 1 Blue Diamond Stakes. (She added the Group 1 Moir Stakes as a three-year-old and all-up won six of 13 starts for more than $1.6 million in prizemoney.)

"Neville Gibson and his pals from the Victoria Club also raced a leg of her. That's how we met, and Neville chaperoned me into the Thoroughbred Club as a member. I have really enjoyed every minute of it, especially the great company."

However, during the past two years Green has struck gold with Almandin and then Rekindling winning the Melbourne Cup.

"Nobody ever expects to win the Melbourne Cup but as luck has it we have won two on end," he said.

"It all started when Nick Williams told Lloyd he would like to involve some friends in their European draft of gallopers. Lloyd warned him that the only way that could succeed was to have the gallopers in Australia, and sound.

"Anyway, we had occupied the box next to the Williams box at Flemington for many years and we were all friends. So, when Nick asked us to go into a batch of 13 internationals, we decided to get involved. As it turned out, one of the horses died and another, Almandin, injured a tendon.

"Eventually Almandin recuperated and was ready to race and Lloyd said that as we were originally involved, we should get the chance to sign up again. So, Barb and I, Brian Singer, Peter Mehrten, John Ingham and his wife, Vinny Sammartino and Michael Gudinski jumped in. Almandin immediately won the Bart Cummings which automatically qualified him for the Melbourne Cup, and next start a month later he won the big one!

"If that was something special, last year was just exceptional"

"If that was something special, last year (2017) was just exceptional. Ridiculous, in fact.

"I was involved in the Melbourne Cup quinella, with a share in the winner Rekindling as well as a slice of runner-up Johannes Vermeer.

"Then we went to Sandown and The Taj Mahal won the Zipping Classic from Almandin, and Villermont won the Sandown Guineas. We also had success with Hell Or Highwater who won the Listed Heatherlie Stakes at Caulfield in the September.

"It was just a freak year, but one I will never forget," he said.

And he didn't have his house on any of them!

THERE have been many occasions when stewards would have come in handy at Thoroughbred Club functions and so it is appropriate that two of the best remain regular attendees.

Pat Lalor, who joined the Victoria Racing Club steward's panel in the late 1950s and retired as chief steward after almost 17 years at the helm, joined as a member the year after his retirement in 1996. "I used to come before that as a guest of Smokey Dawson, but while I was working in an official capacity I didn't think it proper to be linked to any organisation."

Lalor, a former top amateur rider, kept busy after retirement as a consulting steward with Harness Racing Victoria and then was a driving force as honorary treasurer in rebuilding the Healesville Amateur Racing Club back to its former glory.

"I fit in alright: I can handle the characters, some of whom I had dealt with on a professional basis in the past.

"The Thoroughbred Club is a wonderful advertisement for racing, full of characters, contributors and camaraderie"

"I sit with Ron Hutchinson and we have a great chat about the good old days. The club is more about breeders and owners, so a lot of people I was involved with — the trainers and jockeys — are not involved in the club.

"But I've got to meet so many great characters and so many people who love the racing caper during my time that I really look forward to going to every function. The Thoroughbred Club is a wonderful advertisement for racing, full of characters, contributors and camaraderie," Lalor said.

Michael Smith was a highly-respected steward who arrived from Sydney and immediately was nabbed by the Thoroughbred Club as a guest speaker.

"I had been in town only a few weeks and I ended up being a guest speaker at the Hotel Australia. I had a good time, answering all the questions and hopefully shedding some light on being a steward in Australian racing.

"I retired some 30 years ago. I'm 91 now and still get to a lot of functions and really enjoy the company and racing stories that so many members tell to entertain me," he said.

THE THOROUGHBRED CLUB is an important gathering of influential men in the thoroughbred industry and it is fitting that Victoria's most influential racing person, the Racing Minister, was an honorary member.

Neil Trezise, known throughout the land as a distinguished footballer and politician, was one of the most popular men at the club until his death, aged 75, in 2006. He was a champion Geelong rover (premiership player in 1951 and 1952, club captain in 1959) whose career spanned a decade from 1949 and involved 185 games and 272 goals.

After he retired he continued his involvement with the club as a reserves coach, was president of the social club, and, in 1974, became club president.

He was a superstar around Geelong and a natural to represent the area, which he did for 28 years from 1964.

When the John Cain government came to power in 1982 he was made minister for Youth, Sport and Recreation and was the only minister to hold the same portfolio throughout the Cain/Joan Kirner governments, eventually departing in 1992.

As minister for sport he was able to follow his greatest sporting passion — horse racing.

He bred and part-owned multiple city winners including Dark Ruler, a horse trained by his good friend Bob Keirl.

Former Victorian Racing Club chairman Peter Armytage said horse racing had lost a great ally when Trezise died.

"We had a wonderful rapport. Good politicians are scarce, and he was one of them," Armytage said.

Trezise was a shy, unassuming man who never boasted about his footy exploits or his political pull.

In retirement he spent a lot of his time at his 2 hectare property at Leopold, where he once bred horses.

Tom Reynolds stepped into the big shoes of "Nipper" Trezise and brought to the Thoroughbred Club a genuine country charm.

Reynolds, born in Moe, was a farmer from 1953 to 1957, when he became a trainee executive with G. J. Coles. In 1959 he became a shearer and in 1967 a hardware merchant at Romsey. In 1979 he was elected to the Victorian Legislative Assembly as the Liberal member for Gisborne. He was promoted to the front bench in 1982 as Shadow Minister for Sport, Recreation and Racing but stepped down in 1988.

He returned to the position in 1991, and when Jeff Kennett took office, he became Racing Minister, adding the role of Minister for Rural Development in 1996. He retired from politics at the 1999 state election.

THE MELBOURNE RACING CLUB has long supported and sponsored the Thoroughbred Club, most notably with the outstanding facilities of the Caulfield committee dining room for the Blue Diamond Stakes and Caulfield Cup eve gala luncheons. Mike Symons, who stood down on August 1, 2018 as chairman of the MRC after six years as chairman, has enjoyed a long association with both the Thoroughbred Club (a member for more than a decade) and the Melbourne Racing Club, where he has been a member for 25 years and, until his retirement, on the committee for 14 years.

And he has a tangible affiliation with the Caulfield Cup eve luncheon and the great race itself, as he explained when proposing the toast to the club in 2011. "Northerly is one of my favourite horses. I had $20,000 on him at 9/2 so you can understand how much I loved him when he carried 58kg and led all the way to defeat subsequent dual Cox Plate winner Fields Of Omagh, who carried only 55kg, in 2002.

"So much so that I named my son Thomas Northerly.

"I still remember him telling me that he was only a kid, and that at his primary school and he was the only one named after a horse. "I hate it," he'd said as I tried to explain the reasons for his naming and why he had a large photo of Northerly in his room, autographed by Greg Childs, Paddy Payne (who won a Cox Plate on him) and his trainer Fred Kersley.

"I am not sure in my lifetime I will see a better horse than Northerly win the Caulfield Cup. I think it is the best Caulfield Cup ever run," Symons said, adding he may be a tad biased.

"I'm sure Thomas will grow to love his second Christian name, although maybe not as much as I do."

"When you have more than 800 people at a luncheon to celebrate a race, you know you are doing a great job to promote racing"

Symons was introduced to the Thoroughbred Club by MRC committeeman Peter McCarthy "with the idea to get the average age of members under 50."

"The relationship of the MRC with the TBC is really important. We are both passionate about owning, breeding and racing horses. The link is very significant and we at the Melbourne Racing Club treasure it.

"I think an important development has been the introduction of The Colts at the Thoroughbred Club because not many years ago it was looking like an old man's club. The Thoroughbred Club and racing in general needs to look at the next generation and the club has done that.

"The Thoroughbred Club does a great job in promoting racing and getting people active in racing. You see that every year at the Blue Diamond Stakes eve luncheon, and especially the gala Caulfield Cup eve luncheon, where so many owners, trainers, breeders, industry identities, bookmakers and sponsors get together with prominent guests. When you have more than 800 people at a luncheon to celebrate a race the following day — and pay tribute to the previous year's winner — you know you are doing a great job to promote racing.

"I love it and I'm just hoping a horse somewhere near the ability and class of Northerly comes along again."

GARY LECHTE simply loves a galloper he owned named Fendalton. He even named his massive boat after it — and for good reason.

The story began when Lechte bought a yearling by Licorice Stick, who ended up being trained by John Leek Jnr.

"He had a couple of really good trials and then worked sensationally at Breakfast with the Stars at Moonee Valley before the 1989 Cox Plate meeting. In fact, he worked 15 minutes before the start of the morning's official workouts so virtually everyone missed it. Michael Clarke rode it and told me that I should forget the Saturday race and run it in a welter soon after. I quickly figured out he was committed to the Colin Hayes-trained Eastern Classic and couldn't ride Fendalton in the Waterford Crystal Mile. That gave me a huge boost of confidence, knowing that he thought it was going so well but couldn't ride it.

"So, I stuck to the plan and rang Gary Willetts and convinced him to ride it, even though it was 20/1 in *The Herald* that day.

"Anyway, I was at Patterson Lakes marina looking at a boat which was being sold for about $90,000 and I told the bloke that if Fendalton won the Waterford Crystal Mile on the Saturday I'd be back to buy it. He must have thought I was a nutter.

"I went to Moonee Valley full of confidence and told Gary as I was legging him up what sort of sling he was in for if he won. I think he nearly fell off the horse, but he just said: 'leave it to me.'

"I went to the TAB and had $500 each way on the tote. Then I went to two bookies and had $750 each way between them at 100/1 That gave me $1250 each way at more than 100/1.

"Willetts jumped Fendalton to the front from the barriers, led all the way and kicked on the home turn to win by about half-a-length. I was on the grassy area in front of the stand, dad was on the fence and mum was in the grandstand,

and we were going ballistic.

"I received a $15,000 Waterford Crystal trophy — the best trophy I've ever had — along with a dozen Waterford Crystal glasses and then went to collect.

"I hit the TAB first and they wrote me a cheque for $87,000 and then I headed to the bookies who said they could pay me cash or I could wait until next week because they wouldn't write cheques. I took the money and mum and dad and I stuffed it in every pocket (and purse) available. I had more than $150,000 in cash and a cheque for $87,000 and I guess you would say it was a wow of a trip home!

"$150,000 in cash and a cheque for $87,000 and I guess you would say it was a wow of a trip home!"

"The next day the bloke at the marina rang and congratulated me on the win and asked if I was serious about buying the boat and by Monday morning I owned it. On the Tuesday morning I bought a big bunch of roses (for Willett's wife Raewyn) and under them I put in Willett's sling in cash. He told me of all the great horses he had ridden and all the great races he had won, that was the biggest sling he ever received.

"I named my new boat *Fendalton* and when I bought a much bigger one, which is moored on the Gold Coast, I named it *Fendalton*.

"Unfortunately, Fendalton finished fourth, beaten about one-and-a-half lengths, at his next start in the Honda Stakes — by a horse named Better Loosen Up! — and then broke down running in the Railway Stakes in Perth. The irony was that Michael Clarke travelled to Perth to ride him in that race so he missed the boat, so to speak, twice!"

RON HUTCHINSON, former champion jockey and legend of the turf, has become the man with the grand entrance in recent years as he opens the Caulfield Cup eve function by parading that year's cup into the room.

Unhappily, it didn't begin so well, with then president John Connellan getting the Australian Youth Choir to sing the National Anthem — and 850 people totally blanketing his entry!

From then on, he has been granted an unimpeded run!

Hutchie, whose riding career spanned four decades from 1943 to 1979, is one of the most popular and admired club members.

He is well qualified to transport the prized Caulfield Cup into the luncheon each year. As a 17-year-old apprentice he won the 1945 Group 1 Australian Cup on Spectre at 33/1. It was the first of the 60 Cup winners he was to ride in Australia, earning him the nickname of the "Cups King".

Hutchie left for Ireland in 1960 and his first ride in the UK was a win on Martial in the 2000 Guineas for Queen Elizabeth. He then pioneered the practice of light plane travel to ride most days through England, Ireland and Europe, often riding at more than one meeting per day. He then had a retainer to ride for the Duke of Norfolk, for whom he rode successfully for 16 years following the retirement of Scobie Breasley.

During this association his most notable victories included the Ascot Gold Cup, the British Two Thousand Guineas and One Thousand Guineas, along with the Goodwood Cup and the English St. Leger. He also won the Irish One Thousand Guineas on three occasions and the Two Thousand Guineas once.

Hutchie ended his brilliant riding career as the first international rider to be retained by the Singapore and Malaya Turf Club, where he won the 1978 jockeys' premiership. Ron also achieved many other notable firsts during his career. He won the only Olympic Cup on Pandie Sun, held in Melbourne in 1956; he was the first international jockey to ride in Naples in 1964, and he gave one of racing's most influential owners of the past four decades, Sheik Mohammed, his first ever winner on a three-year-old filly named Hatta.

During his career, Ron rode more than 2000 winners in 15 countries — Australia, England, Ireland, Scotland, Belgium, France, Italy, Germany, USA, Spain, Turkey, Malaysia, Singapore, Sweden, and New Zealand.

He was inducted into the Australian Racing Hall of Fame in 2005, and for over 20 years has judged the rider of the "Ron Hutchinson award for riding excellence", for the best rider over the four days of the Flemington carnival.

"Hutchie", as he is better known among his friends, was inducted into the Australian Racing Hall of Fame in 2005 and made a Life Member of the VRC the following year. And he is a treasured member of the Thoroughbred Club since September 19, 1989.

SCOTT WHITEMAN relates a yarn of mixed fortunes with a galloper he part-owned. The eventual dual Group 1 winner Palentino was heading to his first start at Ballarat and Whiteman, then boss of Country Racing Victoria, was running late after inspecting the track at St Arnaud.

"He was $4.20 into $1.80 that day and I was really excited. I was speeding from St Arnaud to Ballarat when I received a call from trainer Darren Weir to say the horse could be vulnerable because he wanted it ridden quietly to help its education.

"I got such a shock by what he said that I slowed down to the speed limit — and over the next hill was a cop with a camera!

"Palentino got beaten and the punters lost but I saved three driving points and hundreds of dollars in fines."

ONE of the contributors and characters of the Thoroughbred Club was Jacob "Yank" Crafti. He was connected to the St Kilda football club — TBC member Gerry Ryan was vice-president to Lindsay Fox — and he owned some good horses, including Father's Day who ran third to Taksan in the 1978 Caulfield Cup.

"He poured a lot of money into the club, was an avid Carlton supporter and nature's gent," according to Ian Scroggie.

"However, one day he had a red-hot go at the Minister for Racing, Tom Reynolds, at our luncheon and was so intoxicated he collapsed and was taken away by ambulance.

"Even his friends turned on him and he was facing the prospect of being expelled from the club. However, he had done so much for so many that I admonished him for his behaviour. I told him to write me a humble and heartfelt apology, which he did, and he sheepishly returned to the fold."

KEVIN O'BRIEN is living his dream on a larger and far more successful scale than he ever intended.

"I'd always wanted to own a small farm with a few broodmares since my childhood when I rode ponies on my father's farm," the former Melbourne Racing Club committeeman said.

O'Brien has been a prominent owner/breeder for decades and his star continues to rise after humble beginnings.

When he was in his early 20s he began a 40-year relationship with trainer Ron Maud.

"My first horse was Fighting Legend, who unfortunately didn't have much fight in him and certainly wasn't a legend," he said.

The breakthrough success for O'Brien came with Gold Edition. He won two Group 1 races, the 2006 Ascot Vale Stakes and the 2007 Manikato Stakes, as well as finishing runner-up in five other Group 1 features behind the ilk of Miss Andretti and Takeover Target. He kept her as a broodmare.

Breeding is the passion that drives O'Brien, especially following the Group 1 wins of Global Glamour in the Flight Stakes at Randwick, and, eight days later running in the other direction, the Thousand Guineas at Caulfield.

O'Brien and his wife Tanith raced the modest mare Spectacula who, when mated with Testa Rossa, produced Global Glamour. That sale propelled the O'Brien breeding establishment, Lauriston Thoroughbred Farm, onto the national stage. "I'd always wanted to own a small farm with a few broodmares and after looking around Alexandra where I came from, we saw a fabulous property at Corinella. We put in a bid but didn't get it. However, as luck would have it, we contacted the agent some time later to ask to look for another property. He said the original deal had fallen through and our dream property was about to go back on the market so we ended up getting it in the end.

"From what started out as a plan to have four or five broodmares on a small farm has turned into looking after 34 broodmares and an extensive staff.

"But I wouldn't swap it for the world."

O'Brien is justifiably proud of Lauriston Thoroughbred Farm, which operates two separate properties near Corinella, 120km south east of Melbourne.

The original holding of 229 acres overlooks the picturesque countryside and silver waters of Western Port Bay. It is a dedicated pre-training and educational facility catering for thoroughbred racehorses of all the ages.

Just 1km away is the second property of 138 acres, purposely developed to accommodate thirty to thirty-five broodmares and their progeny. This facility boasts custom built foaling stables, day yards, a veterinary room, paddocks of varying sizes and a centrally located staff accommodation with a panoramic outlook to each of the surrounding paddocks and scenery beyond.

He also is proud of his association with the Thoroughbred Club, which dates back a dozen years when he was nominated by John Ford.

And he has enjoyed a bit of luck at the traditional Caulfield Cup eve luncheon sweep.

"I had a runner in the 2008 Caulfield Cup and was lucky enough to have another runner courtesy of the sweep.

"When my horse Ice Chariot, a Queensland Derby winner, clearly wasn't going to figure in the finish (eighth), I looked to the front of the field and there was the import All The Good leading the way. I don't know what people around me were thinking of my sudden switch of horses, but I started barracking loudly for All The Good and at least made a dollar out of the result."

O'Brien said "fun and friendship" are the cornerstone of his love of the club "especially for a bloke my age because you can't buy those ingredients in a club dedicated to horses."

DEAN HUMPHRIES, a licensed syndicator and bloodstock agent, knows all about the luck involved in being a winning owner.

He bought a Danehill Dancer filly at the Melbourne Premier Sales for a modest $22,500 and, after rejecting the name Nordic but Nice, the filly raced as Arapaho Miss.

But that was not half as lucky as one lady unwittingly became. As he couldn't syndicate the filly fully, he decided to lease the last share as a door prize at one of his social events. The lucky winning lady walked away with a cheque for $75,000 when Arapaho Miss won the 2007 VRC Oaks.

"Would you believe that after winning the $75,000 I never heard from her again. She wasn't really into horses and didn't give me the chance to follow up with the offer of a small share in another horse. You win some and lose some," Humphries said.

It was not all bad news for Humphries, who sold Arapaho Miss to stud, where she has sired the ilk of stakes winner De Little Engine.

Humphries had an enjoyable season in 2014/15 when he won the Thoroughbred Club owners award. "I was immensely proud to stand up at the Caulfield Cup function to receive the award. It now sits proudly in my office alongside the Oaks trophy."

FEW members of the Thoroughbred Club could match the rush of adrenalin and success enjoyed by the late Ross Herron between 2010 and 2014.

Herron said he simply was in the right place at the right time, when at the 2009 Melbourne Cup, the then TVN director was sitting next to Gai Waterhouse, savouring a big payout on some multiple bets he'd had on the Cup. The trainer — a master promotor and horse seller — was quick to tell him about a promising stayer her husband Robbie recently had bought in New Zealand.

She told Herron that the horse was named after him — Descarado, which she informed Herron, was Spanish for shameless, sassy, cheeky or impertinent.

Herron related the story that before he knew it, the wad of notes flew from his suitcoat pocket into Waterhouse's purse.

"I had a sizeable collect on the trifecta and first four in the Cup. Gai put her hand on my knee, told me she had a Melbourne Cup winner for sale and that it was named after me, and before I knew it the money was out of my pocket and in her handbag," Herron said.

"Before I knew it the money was out of my pocket and in her handbag"

Although Herron had raced many horses and had been involved with five Group 2 winners. Derscarado's Caulfield Cup win was his first at the elite level.

The High Chaparral gelding had won twice and was runner-up twice in New Zealand before Waterhouse took control and it didn't take long for Herron to become excited about the galloper's prospects. As a three-year-old he was runner-up in the Group 2 Tulloch Stakes and Group 1 AJC Derby.

He then won the Group 2 Hill Stakes in September of 2010 before a disappointing run in the Group 1 Turnbull Stakes at Flemington in his final lead-up to the Caulfield Cup — explaining the $17 on offer about his chances.

In Heavy 9 conditions and with only 52.5kg on board, jockey Chris Munce had the gelding in the top three throughout the 2400m race before taking the lead at the 400m mark and staving off Harris Tweed, Monaco Consul and Shocking. "This is the biggest thrill I've ever had. Just don't tell my wife. It's just fantastic," Herron joked after the feature.

Descarado, who returned to Caulfield 12 months later to win the Group 1 Caufield Stakes (2000m) at weight-for-age, eventually succumbed to a leg ailment and was retired in March of 2013. He had earned connections $2.595,583 with his five wins and seven placings from 21 starts.

Herron, however, had no time to lament the loss of Descarado. He already was chasing another dream of winning the Melbourne Cup.

Not that it affected Herron's amazing run of success as he bought into another import, the Irish stallion Fiorente, also trained by Waterhouse.

The first Australian start for Waterhouse was in the Melbourne Cup (3200m) in 2012 and the son of Monsun finished runner-up by a length to the Lloyd Williams-owned Green Moon, having started at $31.

He didn't appear again until the spring of 2013 but won the Group 2 Dato Tan Chin Nam Stakes (1600m) at Moonee Valley, finished third to Shamus Award in the Group 1 Cox Plate (2040m) and then won the Melbourne Cup!

The win, over perennial runner-up Red Cadeaux from the UK, was a triumph for the camp. It was Gai's first Melbourne Cup win, jockey Damien Oliver's fourth success in the race that stops a nation, and Herron's greatest moment in racing.

That was not the end of the road. In the autumn, Fiorente won the Group 2 Peter Young Stakes (1800m) at Caulfield and then the Group 1 Australian Cup (2000m), defeating Green Moon and Shamus Award, two of his previous conquerors. Fiorente sustained a serious tendon injury and was retired to Swettenham Stud in Victoria, owned by Thoroughbred Club vice-president Adam Sangster, after finishing third in the BMW at Rosehill in April of 2014. He had only 20 races for six wins and seven placings.

Herron was part of the final 13 races from the time Fiorente arrived in Australia and he enjoyed four wins and four placings and a share in $6.183 million. During this hectic period of success, Herron also was involved in The Offer, who won the Listed Ballarat Cup (2200m) by almost four lengths on a Heavy 9 in November of 2013 to show he was a superior wet-tracker and, hopefully, another Melbourne Cup candidate the following season.

The son of Montjeu first took on the Sydney autumn carnival and after victories in the Group 3 Manion Cup (2400m) by three-and-a-quarter lengths and the Group 2 Chairman's Handicap (2600m) by two-and-a-quarter lengths on Heavy 9 tracks, he became the Melbourne Cup favourite with a stunning, three-and-three-quarter lengths win in the Group 1 Sydney Cup (3200) on a Soft 5.

However, it was not to be as Melbourne produced Good-rated tracks for the spring. The Offer won only once again, in the Group 3 Bendigo Cup in 2015, ironically on a Good 3 track, before retiring with prizemoney of $1.6 million.

Herron enjoyed a full and fruitful life, but passed away, aged 67, on November 13, 2017. A funeral service at St John's Anglican Church in Toorak attracted a large fraternity of family and friends.

Herron was a charted accountant and former partner at PricewaterhouseCoopers. He was a board member of Kinetic Superannuation Ltd, Select Harvest Ltd and Insurance Manufacturers Australia Ltd. He was also chair of the Board of GUD Holdings and was formerly president of the RACV. He was a director of the RACV between 2007 and 2014, becoming president and chairman in March of 2012. He also was the patron on the Veteran Car Club and was appointed by the Andrews Labor government as one of four eminent Victorians to the Board of the Judicial Commission of Victoria.

And, of course, he was a popular racehorse owner and lively member of the Thoroughbred Club.

GERRY RYAN has pretty much done it all, including winning the 150th running of the Melbourne Cup in 2010 in partnership with another Thoroughbred Club member, Kevin Bamford.

Never one to satisfy himself with just one success in any venture, Ryan then joined forces with Team Williams to snare the 2017 Melbourne Cup with Rekindling. Ryan, OAM, is an Australian businessman, investor, racehorse owner, cycling enthusiast and AFL and rugby sponsor.

The owner and founder of caravan empire Jayco Australia, Ryan also owns Mitchelton Wines with his son Andrew, resorts, the theatrical company Global Creatures and is part-owner of online retailer Bike Exchange.

Ryan, who attended numerous luncheons before becoming a member in 2001, said business eventually forced him to surrender his membership in 2013.

"We had some great luncheons and we had a lot of laughs. And you made plenty of friends. But, in the end, I was just too busy to get to any of the functions, so I let my membership lapse.

"But I retired as chief of Jayco and I am about to give away 20 other businesses so I will have more time to enjoy race meetings and get back into the swing of things," he said, having re-joined the club in 2015.

It is little wonder Ryan had little time to devote to the Thoroughbred Club, given the vast array of businesses he controlled.

And whatever he ventured into, he gave his all — and was fittingly acclaimed. He was one of five inaugural inductees to the Victorian Caravan Industry Hall of Fame in 2012 and was inducted into the Victorian Government's Manufacturing Hall of Fame in 2014 for his contributions to manufacturing excellence.

However, it is sport that ignites a sparkle in Ryan's eye. He is a former board member of the St Kilda Football Club, and for a time owned a partial interest in soccer club Brisbane Roar FC.

Along with Bart Campbell, Matt Tripp and Michael Watt, he has been one of the co-owners of champion NRL team Melbourne Storm since 2013, having been a club director until 2010.

Ryan's interest in cycling began in 1992 when he invested in Kathy Watt, paying for her to attend the Barcelona Olympics where she won two medals.

He has been part-owner and founder of the GreenEDGE Cycling team, currently known as Orica-Scott, the Australian team on the world cycling circuit, and was President of Cycling Australia for a year in 2013.

In 2015 he was an inaugural inductee into the Cycling Australia Hall of Fame. Ryan has been the primary sponsor of the Jayco Australian Opals since 2010, and the women's basketball team Dandenong Jayco Rangers since 1997. In 2013, he was awarded the Australian Olympic Committee's Order of Merit for contributions to sport.

Ryan gives so much support to sports to help others, but it is racing that seemingly is the sole outlet for his personal pleasure.

So, it was a dream fulfilled when Americain, ridden by Frenchman Gerald Mosse, swooped down the outside to coast to a two-and-three-quarter length victory in Australia's greatest race.

Americain, who now stands at the Adam Sangster-owned Swettenham Stud at Nagambie near Ryan's recently sold own horse property, Limerick Lane, and Mitchelton winery where he is building a new stud farm, was an instant success for Ryan and Bamford.

They bought the son of American stallion Dynaformer in 2010 and immediately he won the Group 2 Prix Kergorlay (3000m) in France before heading to Melbourne. He ensured a start in the Melbourne Cup with a narrow win in the Group 3 Geelong Cup.

Starting at $13 and suffering early interference, he finished so powerfully that he left the ilk of Maluckyday, So You Think and Zipping in his wake.

Before heading to stud, he also won the 2011 Moonee Valley Cup (2500m) and Group 2 Zipping Classic (2400m) as well as finishing fourth in that year's Melbourne Cup. He was runner-up in the Group 1 BMW (2400m) and third in the Group 1 Australian Cup (2400m) and fourth in the Caulfield Cup (2400m) of 2012. Ryan certainly didn't need his share of almost $3 million from Americain's career. Success in Australia's most prestigious horserace was all that mattered.

He tried again with another French galloper, Puissance de Lune, who appeared on the scene in 2012. He provided Ryan with the great thrill (and fulfilled ambition) of winning his native Listed Bendigo Cup (2400m) that year by a staggering eight lengths. After the distinctly grey galloper won the Group 3 Queen Elizabeth Stakes (2500m) by a dazzling five-lengths the following start at Flemington, jockey Glenn Boss declared punters had just witnessed the next Melbourne Cup winner.

However, it was not to be as leg ailments curtailed the flashy galloper's career. He dead-heated in the Group 2 Blamey Stakes (1600m) and won the Group 2 Peter Lawrence Stakes (1400m) but five placings in Group 1 features prevented him saluting at the elite level.

Ryan, who is breeding from Americain and Puissance De Lune, will push on. He is building a new stud property at his Mitchelton winery to replace his recently sold stud down the road.

Ryan has a seemingly endless production line of gallopers, many trained by champion trainer Darren Weir, who sport his famous colours of royal blue and white checks, green sleeves and cap on racecourses around the nation.

He joined forces with Lloyd and Nick Williams, club member Alan Green and other prominent owners to share the glory when the four-year-old (only a three-year-old in Europe) Rekindling arrived in Australia and won the Melbourne Cup first-up.

Trained by the young Joseph O'Brien, son of legendary Irish trainer Aidan,

Rekindling started at $15 and ran home strongly to defeat two internationals, Johannes Vermeer and Max Dynamite.

Knowing Ryan, he will not die wondering if another Melbourne Cup will come his way!

RACING can be very much a wing-and-a-prayer caper, so it has been important that several prominent members of the cloth have been associated with the Thoroughbred Club.

One long-time member had no trouble mingling with the club's flock. Father John Brosnan was accustomed to a much tougher crowd as the Pentridge Prison Catholic chaplain for 30 years.

Fr Bros, as he was known universally, reckoned that racing threw up an enthralling gamut of society and, as he often discovered, he ran into so many of his former "inside mates" at the racetrack.

Fr Bros, who died in May of 2003, had a huge appetite for life and greeted everyone with an infectious smile and warm handshake.

He became nationally famous as chaplain to Ronald Ryan, the last man hanged in Australia in 1967. Ryan's last words to him were: "Never forget, no matter how long you live, you were ordained for me."

Fr Bros, who was 83 when he died and was given a state funeral at St Patrick's Cathedral, loved the Geelong footy club and the horses and dogs. His funeral highlighted his ability to mix as an equal with everyone from cabinet ministers to Pentridge inmates.

He was a priest from 1945 until he retired from parish ministry in 1998 and during his vocation he rarely missed an opportunity to watch the Cats or attend a race meeting or a Thoroughbred Club function.

Entertainer Bert Newton, who knew Father Brosnan for more than 40 years, said that Rudyard Kipling "could have written that stuff about walking with kings and retaining the common touch about Bros."

Billy "the Texan" Longley, the Painters and Dockers Union hardman who served 13 years in Pentridge for murder, said Father Brosnan was a much-loved figure in the jail. "He didn't smile, he beamed when he saw you. He used to say to me, "Billy, you skid further on bullshit than on gravel". It was his way of saying violence isn't how to solve things."

Geelong champion Graham "Polly" Farmer, whom Father Brosnan considered the finest footballer he ever saw, might have gone to St Kilda but for Brosnan. "I suppose having a direct phone line to God helped a bit," Farmer said. "He used to joke he couldn't get into the Cudgee reserves even when they only had 17 players."

The late, great *Sun* journalist Tom Prior, who wrote Father Brosnan's biography in 1985, first met the priest as a witness at Ryan's execution. "Ryan returned to his faith just before he died. He said he was saved by a saintly nun and a knockabout priest."

Prior recalled the funeral of a prisoner at which another inmate took exception to Father Bronson's eulogy. "He didn't even believe in God," the prisoner shouted. Father Brosnan replied: "He does now."

Father Joe Giacobbe is another knockabout priest who is a member of the Thoroughbred Club, and, like Father Brosnan, doesn't mind a drink, a chat, a bet and a luncheon.

Fr Joe also knows how the mix with all types, many of whom he meets at race meetings.

In 1972 he set up DOXA, a charitable organisation to cater for disadvantaged youth, and one of his closest associates was the late, great jockey Roy Higgins.

Fr Joe gets around so much that he has the honour of leaving then club president John Connellan speechless before the 2006 Caulfield Cup eve luncheon — a truly momentous moment.

"It happened that I took a trip to Ireland in the 1990s and told a friend of mine, Keith McGowan, that I had booked tickets to see that marvellous Irish comic Noel V Ginnity at the Drury Hotel in Dublin.

"As part of his act, Noel asked if there were any Australians in the room and when I put up my hand, he came down off stage and we had a good chat — I think our mutual mate Keith had been in touch to set it up.

"Anyway, the club invited Noel to be the major attraction at its Caulfield Cup eve luncheon and he was upstairs getting ready and scanning the names on the back of the official program when he said to club president John Connellan: 'I know Father Joe'.

> "John was speechless. I told him God worked in mysterious ways"

"John immediately came downstairs to get me, not believing for a minute that we could know each other. I went upstairs and Noel and I met like long lost buddies and John stood there and said: 'this is bullshit, you two are setting me up.' When it became obvious that we did know each other, John was speechless. I told him God worked in mysterious ways and he should never doubt the spread the church has throughout the world!"

Fr Joe, who knew Henry Harrison well, first went to a Thoroughbred Club luncheon as a guest of Neville Gibson.

"Henry was a very generous foundation member of DOXA and through him, Neville and Laurie Larmer, I went to lots of luncheons before becoming a member in my own right about 15 years ago," Fr Joe said.

"I sat with Albert Millson, another DOXA foundation member, and over the years I have met some wonderful people. This club reflects the racing industry — people from all walks of life getting together for the love of the horse and racing.

"We had been entertained by some outstanding people but my most cherished memory was the ventriloquist Darren Carr who had David Hayes up on stage. David was fantastic, playing along, and I still laugh out loud when I think about it."

FRANK SEDGMAN, the champion former tennis player, is a close friend of Fred Bayne and is a constant companion at club luncheons. He obviously is a stayer

— he is the only man to win the singles, doubles and mixed doubles in the same year at Wimbledon (1952) — because he keeps fronting up at age 90.

Sedgman, along with former Mornington president Murray Horsborough, owned the speed machine Hareeba, trained by Ken Newman, which won among other races the Group 1 Australia Made Stakes and Group 1 Southcorp Stakes, Group 2 Stanley Wootton Stakes, the Group 3 Bobby Lewis Stakes and Group 3 Rupert Steele Stakes — all at Flemington — as well as the Group 2 QTC Cup at Eagle Farm in the mid-1990s.

THE CLUB decided to emulate the Caufield Cup eve luncheon on the eve of the Blue Diamond Stakes in the autumn.

The first took place in 1995, with profits of $20,000 going to Vision Australia. However, after the function raised only $6000 the following year, Vision Australia withdrew. The club then donated profits to the Australian Racing Museum until it transferred from the Caulfield racetrack in 2003.

The function was a joint effort involving the Thoroughbred Club and the VATC (MRC) with members from both clubs taking part.

THE HENRY HARRISON/Thoroughbred Club-VATC Owners Award ran for only seven years and ended when Jonathon Munz completed a hat-trick of wins.

The inaugural trophy went to Woodlands Stud — the Ingham brothers — and then the late Colin Hayes. Having become obvious that the award would stay with the big players or syndication managers, it was decided to confine the competition to club members. The award then went to Ian MacDonald and Jim Racovolis before Munz took control, effectively ending thoughts that the new system would exclude the big players.

The award presentation was included with the VATC presentations to the leading trainer and jockey following the Caulfield Cup barrier draw, then held after the last race in the committee room on the Wednesday's Thousand Guineas day. As that traditional day came to an end, so did the combined Henry Harrison/Thoroughbred Club-VATC Owners Award as the club decided to concentrate on its own TBC Owners Award.

THE CLUB was instrumental in the promotion of Victoria Thoroughbred Country, thanks to the efforts of former member Bernie Armstrong.

It is recognised now on countless number plates on vehicles all over the State. Armstrong was a Geelong Racing Club committeeman who later established the Geelong Thoroughbred Club but its quest for affiliation with the Thoroughbred Club never eventuated.

BALLARAT identity Geoff Robertson was a man of action who enjoyed giving others pleasure. He did exactly that as the owner of Franklin Caravans, allowing tens of thousands of holiday-makers to cruise the nation from the start of the 1950s.

He also owned a 75ft boat, the MV *Iluka*, which he generously launched for Thoroughbred Club members for bay cruises, holding "monthly meetings" aboard in 1982 and 1983.

Robertson, a long-time member of the club, owned many good gallopers and bred many at his Ballarat stud farm. Robertson built his first caravan at the age of 20 in the rear of his father's Town Hall Hotel in Armstrong Street, Ballarat, and many years later he sold the booming business and became a developer in the Ballarat area.

He was inducted into the Caravan Industry Association of Victoria's Hall of Fame in 2015.

"The (Port Phillip) Bay cruises were fabulous aboard the magnificent motor yacht. The yacht also was the venue for a Caulfield Cup eve luncheon after-party!" recalled Ian Scroggie.

"Geoff's generosity will be long remembered."

THE CLUB has attempted to vary speakers, and venues, to engender interest and member support over the years. Major events have been staged at the Hotel Australia, the Southern Cross, Leonda and, mostly, the Caulfield racecourse.

However, for monthly meetings, events have been arranged at race days, nights at the Sandown greyhounds thanks to Harry Harrison and Geoff Dawson, stud visits, brewery visits, trips to Parliament House Members Dining room, the MCG, other sporting venues and restaurants, as well as aboard the motor yacht MV *Iluka*.

COMMITTEEMAN Mike Kostos was instrumental in gaining approval for the Club Honour Board in early 2000, and it was completed and unveiled on July 25 that year by Patron-In-Chief Harry Harrison.

The Honour Board was mounted in the ground floor Members Bar at Caulfield.

MEMBERS enjoyed informal golf days for many years before the event was given calendar status in 1985, co-ordinated by Rupert Legh.

Des Rowe was the official handicapper while Geoff Dawson also was integral to its success.

Stanley Leighton provided everyone with insignia golf balls for many years and Merv Brown stepped up to donate the Members Perpetual Trophy.

The event gave way in 2000 to a Golf Challenge between the Thoroughbred Club and the Carbine Club, both like-minded racing associations.

Thoroughbred Club member Graeme Simmons donated the Gold Perpetual Trophy and the Carbine Club won the inaugural event and repeated the dose the following year at Commonwealth Golf Club.

However, the competition soon faltered when the Carbine Club could not muster sufficient players, and the club no longer has golf on its official agenda.

FOR many years Christmas parties took the form of a family day held at a variety of members' homes or studs and provided entertainment money could not buy.

An ageing membership saw the need for far more creature comforts and in the nineties the Christmas party became more of a cabaret/dinner dance. Henry Harrison held many Christmas parties at his properties at Tyabb and then Pearcedale, and after a period of dinner dances, Gary Lechte opened Delamere in 2000 and 2001 and attracted as big a crowd as ever, with Father Christmas arriving by helicopter.

Geoff Tucker serviced all hardware requirements (marquee and settings), while Dallas Paterson's Dava Lodge serviced all beverage requirements.

Throughout, a constant on the Thoroughbred Club's calendar was a dinner dance to again involve wives and partners of members.

GUEST speakers have come from almost every walk of life, and not always associated with racing.

In 1982, Captain Mark Phillips was the guest speaker at the Caulfield Cup eve luncheon at the Southern Cross Hotel. The husband of Princess Anne was in

International Management Group

Sydney · Cleveland · Brussels · Christchurch · Hong Kong · London · Los Angeles · Milan · New York · Paris · Rio de Janeiro · Tokyo
Suite 1403 National Mutual Centre · 44 Market Street Sydney · NSW 2000 Australia · 02-290-2211 · Telex: AA23703

Mr. H. Harrison
President
Thoroughbred Club of Australia
C/- 37 Cerberus Street
Donvale
Vic. 3111

Dear Mr. Harrison,

I would like to take this opportunity to personally thank you for your kind invitation to the Caulfield Cup Eve Luncheon which I thoroughly enjoyed.

It has been good to be back in Australia this year and I am looking forward to returning in 1983 when we may meet again.

Kind regards,

International Management Group of America Pty. Limited

Australia for a month and to compete in a three-day event at Werribee — which started on Caulfield Cup day!

Among those at the luncheon, and whose photos appeared in *The Herald* the following day, were champion trainers Bart Cummings and Bob Hoysted, club president Henry Harrison, Mick Bicash, *Sporting Globe* racing writer Rollo Roylance and Racing Minister Neil Trezise.

It was reported that the club had 60 members who owned almost 2000 thoroughbreds!

More than 600 guests attended, welcomed by the official party of Trezise, VRC chairman and TAB president Hilton Nicholas, and VATC (MRC) chairman Sir Rupert Clark, along with Harrison.

Bill Collins compered the show and John Russell provided the phantom broadcast.

Mr Trezise included in his speech an aside to Sir Rupert Clark about the white line and fence at Caulfield, a reference to the barriers of the day that segregated the men from the ladies.

The Herald reported that the function was attended by the "who's who in the racing world — top trainers, jockeys, owners, bookmakers and plenty of punters."

Capt. Mark Phillips, through his agent the International Management Group, sent a letter of thanks to the club for an invitation to the event (page 101).

IRISH comedian Noel V Ginnity agreed to be a guest performer at The Thoroughbred Club in 2006 only after John Connellan and Gary Lechte went to extreme lengths to lure him.

Connellan had been a fan of the comedian for many years but he couldn't get the deal over the line because his fee was simply too costly.

"Noel was travelling with a mate who was a dancer in Riverdance and I agreed to run four extra shows at my SkyHigh establishment to balance the books, but we still couldn't get it to work because accommodation was the sticking point," Connellan explained.

"Finally, I said cheekily to Gary Lechte that I had signed Noel to a contract. He said well done, but how did you sort out the accommodation? I said I had put him up at Gary's apartment in Jolimont and Gary didn't bat an eyelid and simply said 'good on you'."

Having told Ginnity how much the club was struggling and negotiating a favourable fee, you can imagine the Irishman's surprise when Lechte arrived at Tullamarine to collect him in his luxurious Rolls Royce Phantom.

"This is unbelievable," he said of the car as his feet dangled from the back seat while his 5ft 2in torso swivelled in all directions admiring the vehicle.

"When it comes to women, three will be plenty!"

When he arrived at Lechte's plush apartment he declared the lounge was "bigger than my house!"

"You have outdone yourselves," he said, before adding: "But when it comes to women, three will be plenty!"

He was a stunning success and is part of an historic photograph which features Hall of Fame trainers Bart Cummings, David Hayes, Lee Freedman and John Hawkes, along with Lechte and Connellan at the function.

THE greatest coup for the club was luring Barry Humphries to a Caulfield Cup eve function. Gary Lechte spent three years negotiating with the Australian legend before he made it to the 2005 event.

"Only five people knew he was the surprise performer and we kept it a huge secret.

"But Barry was such a professional that he decided he wanted to look at the venue the day before to determine how best to tackle his performance. So, I picked him up and we drove to Caulfield. I hadn't made any arrangements to get in and expected nobody to be there," Lechte said.

"To my horror, we drove smack bang into the Garden and Flower Show where thousands of people were roaming the area. People recognised Barry immediately and came rushing up, asking for autographs. He even bought a couple of things. But nobody guessed he was our guest speaker the next day. You could not have orchestrated a better surprise.

"And it took some organising. He was in Sydney on the morning of the luncheon doing a spot on the *Today Show*. So, I had him fly to Tullamarine airport where a helicopter was waiting to zip him to the Caulfield racecourse.

"He'd originally asked for $100,000 to do the show but I kept at him and realised I had him for a massive amount less when I spoke with his manager/producer Harley Medcalf.

"He told me that he'd give me a hint. He said Barry Humphries didn't consider doing the Sir Les Patterson skit as work. It was fun to him because it was so politically incorrect that he rarely had the opportunity to be Sir Les. I played on that and told him he could really let his hair down at the Thoroughbred Club and that Sir Les could do and say what he liked. He loved that idea and we had a deal.

"I must add that I personally went around to speak to the ladies at the function about 30 minutes before Barry Humphries was due to perform and told them individually we had an entertainer who would be rather blue and if they were in any way uncomfortable that they should excuse themselves before he got on stage.

"I told the Master of Ceremonies, Craig Willis, about 20 minutes before showtime that Barry was to perform. That's how big a secret it was. His jaw dropped as I asked him to go upstairs and organise an introduction with Barry," Lechte said.

To this day, Connellan recites the Willis introduction verbatim: "Ladies and gentlemen, I am not qualified to speak about today's guest so let me repeat what others have said about this man. In the words of Australian Prime Minister John Howard, he is one of the greatest Australians ever."

A hush enveloped the room as Craig dramatically shuffled papers and continued. "In the words of the President of the United States of America George

Bush, he undoubtedly is one of the greatest men of the modern era!

There were muffled whispers around the room as Craig continued. "In the words of Pope John Paul, he is one of the greatest humanitarians of our time, and in the words of Mother Teresa, he is the great xxxx I have ever had.

"Ladies and gentlemen, I give you Doctor Sir Lesley Patterson!!!!"

The room erupted as two beautiful girls led Les in — and the club didn't receive one word of complaint about the entire performance," Connellan said.

Lechte picks up the story. "He was spectacular, easily the highest-profile entertainer the Thoroughbred Club has ever had. I gave him some notes to help him be topical, including the fact that the greatest trainer of all time, Bart Cummings, was on the main table directly in front of the stage.

"He was spectacular, easily the highest-profile entertainer the Thoroughbred Club has ever had"

"The trouble was that I had hand-written the names of guests he could refer to, and my hand-writing was never the best. So, Sir Les asked the audience if Barry Cummings was present. Everyone laughed and thought it was part of the act."

Bart was made an Honorary Life Member of the Thoroughbred Club and, of course, was a regular at the Caulfield Cup eve functions.

Over the years he had given great pleasure to many with his one-liners.

Q: "What to do you attribute your success to?"

A: Horses.

Q: "What did you say to Darren Beadman when he told you God had spoken to him and he was quitting race riding to study to become a religious minister?

A: I think you should get a second opinion.

Q: What did you say when told by a health inspector that there were too many flies at your Adelaide stables?

A: How many am I allowed?

However, this time the 12-time Melbourne Cup-winning trainer and seven-time Caulfield Cup-winner wasn't sure if he was the butt of a joke or part of a Sir Les stuff-up. And neither were the 800-plus guests in the room.

As an aside, John 'Dr Turf' Rothchild was on the balcony having a cigarette when someone said that a Barry Humphries impersonator had just walked on stage and was pretty good. Rothchild couldn't believe it when he returned and realised it was Barry Humphries on stage.

The inadvertent mix-up worked so well that Rothchild went on radio the following day, Caulfield Cup day, and referred to every entrant from the Cummings stable as being trained by Barry Cummings.

GARY LECHTE was never bashful about seeking quality entertainers for the Caulfield Cup eve function. He approached American comedic guru Jerry Seinfeld in 2008, 2009 and 2010.

Lechte googled Seinfeld's sister, Carolyn Liebling, and made contact, having had no luck with contact information for his manager or publicist.

Carolyn passed on the information to Seinfeld's management and a series of emails followed, unfortunately to no avail.

"I targeted him because he was a super entertainer who didn't need the big money. He performed because he loved it. Like many others, he was so good that he was just happy to perform, not seek big money like those on the way up demand.

"Naturally I tried to lure him with some slick PR. I told him that Noel V. Ginnity had interrupted a major gig in Ireland to be our previous guest speaker and that Barry Humphries has been the guest before him.

"Unhappily, he just couldn't arrange his itinerary to be in Australia — one year he was making a movie and on the other two occasions he was heavily booked at that time — but it was fun and challenging to try," Lechte said.

Lechte and the committee rejected Sir Michael Parkinson when he wanted a $75,000 appearance fee, but he tried Stevie Wonder and, in 2008, Rolf Harris. He even tried Billy Connolly. "You never know who you can snare unless you give it a go," Lechte said.

He was not always on a winner. One year he organised a Beatles cover band which was an unmitigated disaster, and another year (with the help of Connellan) he arranged Scared Weird Little Guys, who also were a disappointment. However, when Lechte retired as president and handed the reins to Connellan, the bar was at an exceptional height.

He won immediate applause for snaring Darren Carr, the ventriloquist who used David Hayes as his "dummy" in one of the funniest skits ever seen at the Thoroughbred Club luncheon.

"I think that success led to my downfall because the fabulous success of Carr the ventriloquist led me to booking another, the international star David Strassman.

Connellan still cringes when he recalls the performance of the expensive US puppeteer/ventriloquist whose act, involving Ted E Bare, Chuck Wood and Grandpa Fred and Co, came with a MA rating.

"An unmitigated disaster," Connellan confessed. "I'll never live it down."

"But to be fair, I did go on to book Vince Sorreti, Ahn Doh and Peter Dee so one failure wasn't so bad."

The Caulfield Cup eve Thoroughbred Club luncheon has such a high level of performer expectation that any show that is not top-notch gets a rubbishing. At one end of the spectre is Barry Humphries and at the other is David Strassman.

HALL OF FAME trainer Lee Freedman was reluctant when asked by Gary Lechte to give the toast to the Caulfield Cup but relented and provided an emotional and inspirational speech.

"I told him he was underestimating himself," Lechte said of the four-time Caulfield Cup and five-time Melbourne Cup-winning trainer.

"His speech was outstanding. So much so that his biggest rival, David

Hayes, told me his performance was fantastic and that he didn't want to ever be a guest speaker because he couldn't possibly be as good as Freedman."

For a hardened trainer who had trained so many champions, his toast was spellbinding, especially when he recalled the feats of grand galloper Mummify.

"All four of my Caulfield Cup winners were different. Mannerism (1992), Paris Lane (1994) and Doriemus (1995) were super for different reasons.

"But in 2003 Mummify ran them into the ground, leading from start to finish. He ran down the track the following year before the 2005 Caulfield Cup."

Mummify was in front with only 30 metres to run but went down by a short neck and a short neck to Railings and Eye Popper, only to buckle shortly after the finish line.

"His crying out in pain and his ultimate destruction will live with me forever"

The galloper had fractured the sesamoid bone in his near foreleg and had to be put down. Freedman explained how he ran from the mounting yard to be with his warrior, ordered that he not be put down immediately but sent to nearby vets in the hope of saving him.

Mummify had given his all as usual, Freedman said, coming from barrier 17 with top-weight of 57kg, and almost staved off his last two challengers.

"The aftermath of that race still haunts me. His horrific injuries, his crying out in pain and his ultimate destruction will live with me forever," an emotional Freedman told the hushed crowd.

"He was a fighter but could not be saved and we buried him upright in the tradition of old Indian warrior horses at Anthony Freedman's property at Merricks. He was an iron horse," Freedman said.

Only two years earlier, Mummify led all the way from barrier 13 to salute in the Caulfield Cup (with Makybe Diva fourth) to clinch one of his five Group 1 career wins. He also won the SA Derby (2500m) and Underwood Stakes (1800m) in 2003, the Caulfield Stakes (2000m) in 2004 when downing Grand Armee and Starcraft and capped off his career with victory in the Singapore

International Cup. Besides his great record in the Caulfield Cup, Freedman trained five Melbourne Cup winners, four Golden Slipper winners and two Cox Plate winners — and the ilk of Super Impose, Makybe Diva, Alinghi, Mahogany and a host of other champions.

He was also able to capture the Melbourne metropolitan trainer's premiership on seven separate occasions and in 2003 he was inducted into the racing hall of fame.

To cap off an exceptional career, he trained Miss Andretti in the 2006-7 season to win four Group 1 sprints — the Manikato Stakes, Lightning Stakes, Australia Stakes and Newmarket Handicap before, on June 19, he took her to Royal Ascot in the UK to win the Group 2 King's Stand Stakes in course record time.

The Thoroughbred Club was certainly grateful Freedman reluctantly accepted the challenge of toasting the Caulfield Cup in 2006.

ONE of the highlight luncheons involved David Hayes, who upstaged the exceptional ventriloquist Darren Carr.

Hayes, who was enduring a rare lean patch as he put all his efforts into establishing a new base at Euroa, was not keen to be "the dummy" for the act but it proved to be a masterstroke.

"Carr opened by asking David what work he did and David replied he 'used to train winners'. Then he asked where he lived, and David said Euroa because he was too embarrassed to say Toorak.

"From then on Carr took over as the ventriloquist and David lurched around the stage, laughing (in Carr's high-pitched voice) and providing one of the most memorable and hilarious scenes you could wish for at a Caulfield Cup eve function," recalled Leckte.

"I remember looking across the room and Gai Waterhouse was buckled over, tears of laughter rolling down her cheeks. Everyone loved it and David said later that he had more good wishes from people after that than any response to

"Gai Waterhouse was buckled over, tears of laughter rolling down her cheeks"

anything else he had ever done."

And, as we all know, he fixed Euroa and burst back into the headlines again soon after with a flurry of classy winners.

In fact, the Thoroughbred Club has laid claim to being instrumental in the re-making of the David Hayes empire and success.

In 2017, the Hall of Fame trainer reluctantly agreed to toast the Caulfield Cup at the race eve gala luncheon. He had four runners — Harlem ($9), Ventura Storm ($12), He's Our Rokkii ($101) and Boom Time ($51) — and spoke honestly about all after reminiscing about the Hayes family involvement in the great 2400m handicap.

"But I want to warn you — Boom Time is well over the odds. I certainly hope he wins because I own him!" were words that many gleaned from his speech with considerable financial benefit!

ANOTHER special toast came from broadcasting legend Bruce McAvaney, whose statistical knowledge intrigued the audience in 2003.

McAvaney rattled off winner after winner of the Caulfield Cup, no notes, as he scooted unfalteringly from one historic race to the next, one champion to the next.

McAvaney started his illustrious sports broadcasting career calling greyhounds and horse races — including four Melbourne Cups — and remains an avid student of the turf.

His impeccable research allowed him to recount numerous historical yarns and statistics. He plucked out the highlight of Poseidon winning the first of his successive Caulfield Cups in 1906 — the first horse to do so — and a feat achieved only once since — by Rising Fast in 1954-55.

He described what he called the "golden era" between 1920 and 1930, which produced such winners as Eurythmic, the West Australian champion who won 31 races, including 21 at weight-for-age, from 47 starts.

During that decade, Whittier won the Caulfield Cup twice (1922 and 25) and the barrier rogue Manfred had 60kg in his 1926 success.

The "Roaring 20s" were also famous for the burning down of the grandstand on the eve of the 1922 Cup, reputedly by the notorious criminal Squizzy Taylor. Nonetheless, McAvaney pointed point, the race went ahead and was won by Whittier, owned by VATC (Melbourne Racing Club) committeeman Ben Chaffey, much to the cost of bookies.

McAvaney said the 1960s was a "special" time for this Adelaide born-and-bred youngster, inspiring his interest in horse racing.

"I was born in 1953 and was too young to know about Tulloch (1957), but Sometime (1963), Yangtze (1964) and Galilee (1966) were all trained in Adelaide."

He knew that Sometime was trained by Les Patterson only because Bart Cummings was serving a 12-month suspension; that Galilee started at 14/1 despite great lead-up form, and that Yangtze was the first Caulfield Cup winner to lead all the way.

He even found fun in the ride of Shane Dye on Veandercross when runner-up to Mannerism in the 1992 Caulfield Cup.

"What do Shane Dye and (Olympic rower) Sally Robbins have in common? They never said sorry!"

THE CLUB has been blessed to have been entertained by some outstanding comedians or guest speakers, such as the irreverent Sam Kekovich, Brian Doyle and John Garfield.

Kekovich, the former North Melbourne footy champ cum professional speaker, used his vocabulary to bamboozle members while promoting his Lamb campaign and savagely attacking those who wished to demean the

Australian way-of-life. Doyle, the amiable Irishman with a whimsical style, performed with the weight of the world on his shoulders to hilarious effect, while the late Garfield was one of Australia's most decorated comedians who remains a favourite appearance with many members.

Others deserve a special mention for their performances. Vince Sorrenti, a five-time winner of the Mo Award for excellence in comedic performance, played upon his Italian heritage with many jokes, but his trademark line was: "We came, we saw, and we concreted."

And Vietnamese-born Anh Do told the audience that "my mother was so into cooking that for a long time I thought my name was 'taste this'."

THE THOROUGHBRED CLUB introduced The Colts in 2016 in a bid to entice the next generation of members to the club.

For those under 40-years-of-age, The Colts numbers were limited to 20 and unsurprisingly the sons of five prominent members joined, along with the grandson of Kevin O'Brien.

The 14 Colts currently in the club are Danny Barrett, Josh Blanksby, Chris Blomley, Daniel Clohesy, Kane Devitt (son of Peter), Aaron Fisher (son of Cameron), Richard Ford (son of John), Tom Frazer, Simon McCarthy, Lachlan MacDonald (son of Ian), Cameron Menzies (son of Rod), Ben O'Shea, Jack Newton and Michael Walton (grandson of Kevin O'Brien).

New chief executive of the Melbourne Racing Club, Josh Blanksby, said he enjoyed "wearing two hats" as MRC chief executive and a Colt member at the Caulfield Cup eve luncheon.

"The great thing about the club is the diversity of businesses and interests of members. I think it is great the club puts a list of members on the back of the program: when you read down that list you are amazed at the names you recognise and what varying involvement they have in the racing industry.

"Everyone I've met has been welcoming and straight up-and-down people. I'm really happy to become part of the club," he said.

Blanksby, of course, knew many members (and guests) before joining as a Colt. Before he was appointed chief executive of the Melbourne Racing Club in December of 2017, he served as Executive Director of Racing & Corporate Affairs, after a stint as General Manager of Legal & Corporate Affairs at Caulfield. He previously was the Director of Legal and Corporate Affairs at Betfair.

Frazer, who runs his own digital advertising business, is the best mate of Arron Fisher and said they joined immediately the Colts was established.

"Arron and I had been going to the luncheons for about six years before the Colts. We love the club because we come from an era in which younger people are not going to the races like the previous generations.

"We have grown up going to the races and the club gives us the opportunity to talk to people in the racing game, as well as people who are successful businessmen. It is great for networking.

"But importantly we can carry on the legacy from our dads' era. It is not just about us: it is bringing our friends into the club as well to foster the next generation of club members who love horses and racing," he said.

MAX WILLIAMS has been a member of the Thoroughbred Club for only five years, but he already had a host of friends within the club before he joined.

Two of them are Mark Read and Neville Gibson.

Williams spent 20 years as PR for the TAB before owning the Retreat Hotel for three years and then spending three years as the St Kilda football club social club manager. He then ran the Victoria Club for 20 years and spent seven years looking after the wonderful charity DOXA.

He relates the story of the night he had a party at his East Brighton home.

"I was into tropical fish at the time and had a giant fish tank in the middle of the room, a real centrepiece. On the morning of the party I decided that more fish would be a special touch for the party, so I went out and paid about $500 for some really exotic fish.

The party was typical of a racing gig — owners, punters, breeders, bookies and racing writers and everyone had more than their fill of alcohol.

"I woke up the next morning with a raging headache and staggered into the lounge room only to see that red wine had been spilled into the fish tank and all the beautiful exotic fish were floating belly-up on the surface.

"Mark owned up to it, not that it did the fish any good!

"I'd known Mark for years and in early January of 1982 he rang and asked if I wanted to go to Sydney the next day and help with a bit of business. I had just returned from a hot and uncomfortable Christmas holiday, so I said no.

"I have wondered ever since how my life could have changed had I said yes"

"I have wondered ever since how my life could have changed had I said yes: the reason for the invite was to back Getting Closer at 100/1 to win the Domain Stakes at Canterbury in one of the biggest stings in racing history."

Williams also remembers his first encounter with club stalwart Neville Gibson. "He was on the board of DOXA when I joined up and he told me I had two days to get the place sorted. Happily, things worked out well and we became close friends.

"When he had smart two-year-old Samaready with Mick Price, I suggested we backed it well in advance for the Blue Diamond. We got 25/1 and she started at 6/4 and won the big race.

"I was in the outer in a pair of pink shorts and pink T-shirt and when I looked into the mounting yard after the race and saw Neville I couldn't help but jump up and down and carry on like a madman.

"Then Mike Symonds, the Melbourne Racing Club chairman, saw me and asked if I would like to join the owners in the winners' bar to celebrate the victory. I fair-dinkum jumped the fence and, in pink shorts and T-shirt, marched into the inner sanctum and had a ball.

"You can't put a price on the friendships you make in this game, and Mark and Neville are two of the best blokes you could meet," Williams said.

THE Thoroughbred Club can take much of the credit for the establishment of the Thoroughbred Racehorse Owners Association (TROA) which has enjoyed a huge impact on the Victorian racing scene.

TROA was founded out of the Thoroughbred Club. Driving the formation was the pressure on the Club's numbers to accommodate people with common racing interests. Then President of the Thoroughbred Club, Harry Harrison, piloted the Owners Association and was a dominant player from inauguration.

TROA was formed following a meeting of 26 racehorse owners at the Hotel Australia on April 23, 1974.

The inaugural chairman was Geoffrey Bellmaine with Harrison as vice-chairman. The first committee members were Dom Dimmatina, Kevin Heffernan, Tom Trevaskis and Monty Millson.

All six founding gentlemen were prominent members of the racing fraternity as owners and from the beginning set out to ensure fellow owners were protected.

The committee was joined immediately by 34 foundation members.

Bellmaine served as chairman between 1974 and 1976, followed by Dimmatina for the next two years. Harrison then chaired TROA from 1978-1984.

Other presidents have been Gerald Cunningham (1984-87), Nick Columb (1987-2001), David Lauritz (2001-2005), Martin O'Connor (2005-2006), David Moodie (2006-2009), Andrew Lafontaine (2009-2012) and Jonathan Munz from 2012 to the present time.

In 1987, Henry Harrison, Geoffrey Bellmaine, Kevin Harrison and John Dillon were the first TROA members to be awarded life membership. These gentlemen contributed an enormous amount to racing over a long period of time, and John Dillon continued to contribute as the chairman of the Melbourne Racing Club.

Today TROA, which hands out owner badges to those who own race horses and which has been heavily involved in the VOBIS Gold bonus system, plays a crucial, public role in Victorian racing.

ANDREW PEACOCK, who won a Caulfield Cup with Leilani in 1974, was a club member who had more pressing obligations in Canberra as a member of Parliament. However, he never failed to send his apologies, naturally on official Australian government letterhead.

He did so in 1982 when the Minister for Industry and Commerce, and again the following year when Leader of the Opposition.

And for those old enough to remember: Jim Shannon conveyed his apologies on an international telegram!

THE COST of running the Thoroughbred Club in the early days was the sole responsibility of the members, given there was no sponsorship.

Times have changed, and along with them the actual cost of running an event. Take, for example, a letter dated May 1981 from Mrs Jillian Efron, the director of sales at the Leonda by the River. She responded to a club request for a menu and costing to run the Caulfield Cup eve luncheon for 450 guests in the ballroom.

MENU:
Nuts, chips & olives.
Whiting Meunier.
Roast chicken Leonda or Roast sirloin of beef served with garden fresh vegetables.
Apple strudel and cream or strawberries & cream.
Cheese Platters.
Coffee and Chocolate mints.

The cost was $16 per person, plus $8 per table for cheese platters. Without dessert, and including cheese platters, the cost was $15.50 per person. That sure looks cheap at today's prices!

MINISTER FOR INDUSTRY AND COMMERCE
PARLIAMENT HOUSE
CANBERRA, A.C.T. 2600

Hon. Andrew Peacock, MP, is unable to attend the next Monthly Meeting of the Thoroughbred Club of Australia on Tuesday, November 16, as the Parliament is sitting on that day. Could you please convey his sincere apologies.

25th October, 1982.

THE CLUB decided to promote its own label on wine bottles in 1981 when vintner Maurice Bourne of Seymour Vineyards convinced the club to sell his wines. Members could buy a dozen Rhine Reisling bottles, a limited edition with the Thoroughbred Club logo, for $41 a dozen, while a dozen 1979 Cabernet Merlot Malbac or a dozen Vintage Port cost $45 a dozen.

Also, for $45 a dozen, members could purchase a Special Pack "A" of six whites, four reds and two ports, or Special Pack "B" of four whites, four reds and four ports. The offer was generous but, given some members of the club had connections with other wineries, complaints poured in and the scheme did not last.

IN 1982, the club consisted of 55 members, plus five from interstate, six who were honorary members and one honorary life member. The committee decided to consider increasing the membership ceiling to 60 as it had "several nominations in hand" including John Dillon Junior (later club president), William Vass, Maurice Bourne, William Kollosche, Peter Cornell "and others mentioned in passing."

Finances were tight even then, with the annual report showing receipts of $29,944 and expenditure of $30,153, leaving a balance of $4,306.

Of concern to the committee was the cost of the Christmas party — up from $1460 to $2130, and the impending cost increase of a standard monthly luncheon from $10.50 to $15 per head.

By 2001, club membership had risen to 108, with two overseas members, six interstate members and six life/honorary members.

And all but two meetings during the year were held at Caulfield, ostensibly because of the sponsorship arrangements between the two clubs.

The meeting was informed that arrangements that were in place with the VATC/Heath Function Centre (read Melbourne Racing Club and Caulfield Glasshouse Tabaret) provided the Thoroughbred Club with a discount on functions would continue at a similar level of support to the previous year.

Club secretary of the time, Ian Scroggie, said one of the problems associated with the Caulfield Cup eve function at Caulfield was fending off complaints from members about their table position.

"We had 640 people at our 2001 luncheon, a similar number to the previous year, and table arrangements were always a headache. Naturally the official tables were in prime position, but to be fair to every member who organised a table, we had to rotate placements to try to keep everybody happy.

"We tried to spread the tables on the extremities of the room to cover all members while bringing close up coverage of the event to everyone on closed-circuit televisions.

> "I think I had more complaints over table placements than any other issue at the club"

"And I can only imagine what it is like now with more than 800 attending the luncheon! As ever, you can't please everybody all the time and I think I had more complaints over table placements than any other issue at the club.

"But for all that, we had a pool of $21,900 for the sweep, organised by Tony Ongarello, the former champion Fitzroy footballer and VATC committeeman.

"Ongarello was the prime mover behind the sweep, which continues to attract a big pool and great interest among the members and guests."

CLUB member and bloodstock agent John Ford was lucky enough to be involved in two big wins at the Caulfield Cup eve sweep in the early 1990s.

In 1992 my father Frank and I were invited to the luncheon by our good friend and client Albert Millson and sat at a table with club member Geoff

Robinson and his guests from Ballarat.

"When the time came to buy tickets in the Caulfield Cup Sweep the others on the table began to purchase tickets on their own account, unlike when dad and I were previously guests of Merv Brown when tickets were bought by the table and everyone shared the winnings.

"I suggested we buy two $10 tickets each, but rather than looking for change of $50, we bought five. That ticket was drawn out and we had Mannerism running for us in the Cup.

"In the true fashion of a 'horse dealer', he would think about it overnight"

"About 30 minutes later Dr Jack Kennedy approached dad to see if we would sell the ticket. Kennedy was sitting at his table with Barrie Griffiths, the owner of Mannerism, who had sent him over on a mission to buy the Mannerism ticket. Frank, in the true fashion of a 'horse dealer', told Kenney he would think about it overnight and call him in the morning with a decision.

"It had started to rain at Caulfield after the luncheon and continued during the night and we knew that Mannerism could handle a wet track. So, Frank rang Jack Kennedy and said thank you but no thank you to the offer.

"The rest is history with Mannerism, ridden by Damien Oliver, winning the 1992 Caulfield Cup by beating Veandercross, ridden by Shane Dye, in a photo finish. The following year I became a member of the Thoroughbred Club of Australia after being nominated by Albert Millson, and I had my own shared table at the 1994 luncheon.

"We were lucky enough to draw Paris Lane in the sweep. As I entered Caulfield from the members' car park on raceday I ran into Paris Lane part-owner Andrew Ramsden and wished him luck. He just said get in the queue to collect because Paris Lane will win. He surely did, and my table members were very happy with the sweep and the subsequent windfall."

Ford, of course, has bought and sold many horses over decades in the industry, but he will always cherish his connection with 1978 Caulfield Cup winner Taksan. "It all began in the Members carpark at Flemington on Derby Day of 1977 when Monty and Albert Millson, my father Frank and me, along with Merv Brown and our friend and client Pat Samuel from New Zealand were discussing the chances of buying a Cup prospect for the following year.

"Over the journey we had supplied Samuel hurdlers and steeplechasers for the Queen Mother — The Champ, So And So and Sunrama were all top class jumping horses — and during lunch and over a few drinks my father mentioned that Samuel and his brother Peter had a promising young stayer named Taksan, who had won 5 races in New Zealand and was showing good staying potential with the aim to put him over the jumps and an overseas sale.

"Anyway, we ended up doing a deal for Monty and Albert Millson and Merv Brown to buy 50 per cent of Taksan, with Pat and Peter Samuel retaining the other half.

"The horse went to Tommy Smith and the dream of three Thoroughbred Club Members — Monty and Albert Millson and Merv Brown — of winning a Caulfield Cup came true," Ford recalled.

Ford was one of Australia's leading polo players in his younger days, even playing with Prince Philip and Prince Charles in Australia during royal tours. He was captain of the successful Yarra Glen and Lilydale Polo Club and played international polo in Singapore, Malaysia and the Philippines.

He has made many friends along the journey but has a special memory of the late Allan Whittenbury who purchased his first broodmare, named Dealing, from him and his father.

"Whittenbury became a successful racehorse owner and breeder, and one day I noticed a story in a NSW breeding magazine referring to Allan as 'the most astute thoroughbred breeder south of the Murray'.

"When I told Allan about this title he was most pleased. Often, at Thoroughbred Club meetings or with fellow racehorse owners or breeders at the races or bloodstock sales, he would ask me, with a glint in his eye, to repeat the title given to him in the NSW breeding magazine. Allan always enjoyed the comments and the reactions that followed!"

TONY CAVANAGH has been an integral part of the Thoroughbred Club, especially through his association with the Group 1 Blue Diamond Stakes.

The bloodstock agent has not missed Victoria's premier two-year-old feature since the first running in 1971 when Angus Armanasco trained Tolerance to victory. Cavanagh has had an even more tangible association with the race — he bred and raced Let's Get Physical who saluted in 1985 for his mate Robert Smerdon.

Smerdon well remembers Let's Get Physical. "He won at Werribee, then Moonee Valley and then the Prelude and eventually the Diamond all in 31 days. Gee he was a good, tough galloper," Smerdon recalled.

Cavanagh and Smerdon have a long history. "I knew him when he was a jockey and when he started training at Ballarat I did my best to give him horses and to attract clients to his stables," he said.

When Let's Get Physical won the race, Cavanagh had the diamond made into a necklace which his former wife wore to every Diamond day. Now Cavanagh's daughter, Georgie, is carrying on the tradition.

Cavanagh has had an enduring influence on the race.

He bred the mare Irma in 1987 and she is the third dam of Miss Gidget who contested the Diamond a couple of years ago.

In 1990, he bought the mare Imposing Life who dropped Miss Prospect, the dam of 2009 Diamond winner Reward For Effort.

Cavanagh has enjoyed a lifetime involvement in racing. He is a Group 1 winning owner-breeder, former stud owner, Thoroughbred Breeders' Victoria Life Member and a foundation member in 1988 of the Federation of Bloodstock Agents Australia.

Cavanagh's racing impact began as assistant secretary of the Victorian Racecourses Licences Board in the late 1960s before he joined Wright Stephenson in 1970 where he soon became head of the pedigree department when champion sires such as Better Boy and Showdown ruled the roost in Victoria.

He was also on the original sub-committee that commenced grading black-type racing in Australia. He has bought and sold many stars, including Emancipation and Oenjay Star among them.

Cavanagh has bred and raced numerous top-class gallopers over the years, starting with Manchu Prince in 1970 and highlighted by Let's Get Physical. Recently he purchased a half-share for his friend and client Rod Menzies in smart filly Agent Pippa, who at her third start won the Group 3 Gimcrack Stakes (1100m) at Ascot.

"It is behind the scenes that he has accomplished two significant milestones for racing"

However, it is behind the scenes that he has accomplished two significant milestones for racing.

In August of 1992 he helped establish the Victorian Thoroughbred Racing Industry Employers (VICTORIE) group which laid out a business plan for racing, presented to Jeff Kennett just before he became Premier of Victoria. That document led to the Victoria Racing Club relinquishing its administrative role over Victorian racing and the establishment of Racing Victoria.

In the late '70s he joined forces with Mark Read to kick start syndications, which are prevalent today. And in 1989 he opened trade between Australia and Argentina, buying fillies and mares.

Cavanagh has been involved in racing for more than 50 years, but his life doesn't revolve wholly and solely around horses. A firm believer that participants should have other interests outside the industry, he has been an Australia Day Ambassador for the past seven years and has close ties in the art, entertainment and football worlds.

That role began at Coleraine-Glen Thompson in 2012 followed by Edenhope-Harrow (2013), Horsham-Natimuk (2014), Stawell (2015), Wycheproof (2016), Bannockburn (2017) and Ballarat (2018).

YOUNG member Levi Kavanagh well remembers his first foray into racing at Caulfield. The son of leading trainer Mark travelled from South Australia to watch the 2005 Blue Diamond Stakes.

"I backed my dad's horse Undoubtedly and won $8000. I thought: 'How long has this been going on?'

"It was not long before my 21st birthday and we had the wildest party you could imagine."

> **"I backed my dad's horse and won $8000. I thought: 'How long has this been going on?"**

Levi joined the Thoroughbred Club on New Year's Day of 2017 and knows how to enjoy himself — usually with his father as his premier guest!

Levi, who took out his own trainers licence in 2015 but still works as assistant to his father, has worked with horses his whole life, having grown up on the family racing farm at Mount Gambier.

He became a strapper/stable hand in Adelaide when he was a teenager and his love for the thoroughbred grew.

Whilst completing a double degree (Commerce and Marketing) at the University of Adelaide, Levi stepped away from the early morning hours of the stable environment and spent a lot of time at the horse sales. He gained extensive experience purchasing quality horses from leading Bloodstock agents, renowned veterinarians and his father. He also gained valuable insight whilst working brief stints for Magic Millions.

After graduating from University, Levi lived in England for two years where he experienced European stables, racing and sales. Despite his racing background, he envisaged his future in finance and banking.

"I realised over there I really missed it. Sometimes it takes a little bit of time for you to walk away to understand that you were comfortable in what you were originally doing."

So, when he returned to Australia, he re-joined his father at Flemington as assistant trainer before taking over the Morphettville satellite stables where he had considerable success with 20 horses.

THE KRUGER family from Queensland has a special place in the Thoroughbred Club history. Father Merrell and sons Jeff and Griffin are all interstate members with a link to club membership dating back to 1987.

Merrell, owner of Lyndhurst Stud in Queensland, joined the club 31 years ago after attending a couple of Caulfield Cup eve luncheons with his Melbourne-based mate David Marchment.

His sons Jeff and Griffin joined the club in 1997, although they have difficulty attending because of the breeding season at Caulfield Cup time.

Merrell has been involved with breeding since his father Percy and uncle Ted Kruger bought Lyndhurst Stud in 1956. Merrell was studmaster in the early days and stepped up when Percy and Ted split in 1975, leaving Merrell and his father (and now sons) in total control of the famous establishment.

They also owned a sawmill at Ipswich, the biggest in the southern hemisphere. "We made handles for shovels and hammers, for anything and everything. Our slogan was 'We will handle you right'. It certainly grabbed attention," Merrell said.

While still studmaster, Merrell took a huge punt and decided to import the first son of a stallion called Northern Dancer, who at that stage had not established himself as the best Sire of Sires the world has ever seen. Grand Chaudiere became Australia's leading sire of winners in 1980-81 and in his stud career produced 455 individual winners of more than $6 million. He was particularly successful with siring quality broodmares — Snippets is the result of Lunchtime being mated to Grand Chaudiere's daughter, Easy Date.

Lyndhurst Stud, which is set on 2500 acres of prime Darling Downs land and has up to 500 thoroughbreds on the property during peak breeding season, was successful from the outset.

Their initial stallion, Smokey Eyes, was for almost a decade the leading Sire of winners for the whole of Australia. Whilst Smokey Eyes produced many great horses, he produced one filly — who then, and to this day, — has left an indelible mark on Australian racing.

Raced by the Kruger brothers, Eye Liner as a two-year-old had won eight consecutive races — seven by margins of between 6 and 10 lengths. She was taken to Sydney and won the Champagne Stakes (1200m) at Randwick, beating the record held by champion Todman when running 1:9.9.

BILL MILLICAN knows a good thing when he sees it so after a long and quenching taste of the Thoroughbred Club he decided to open a chapter branch on his home turf on the Gold Coast.

Millican had been a regular guest of Albert Millson at the Caulfield Cup eve functions for almost two decades — and continues to frequent the Cup eve function — in his role as a committeeman and then president of the Gold Coast Turf Club.

"A group of us would come down to Melbourne to hand out Magic Millions catalogues and speak to owners and trainers to urge them to come to the Gold Coast. Albert Millson was a great help and he invited me to the Caulfield Cup eve luncheon," Millican said.

"This went on for years and I still come down every year with a small group and have a great time. We attend the luncheon on Friday and the Cup the next day and then fly home on the Sunday. It is one hectic but always memorable weekend. Anyway, after 19 years on the board of the GCTC the time came when my five-year presidency came to an end and I decided to stand down. I didn't think it was fair to stay on the board as the past president while a new president was making his way in the post.

"It was then that Gary Lechte, who was Thoroughbred Club president at the time, and other committee people suggested I start up a Thoroughbred Club on the Gold Coast. It was 2007 and I kicked it off as president and have been running it ever since," he said.

To celebrate, Lechte, John Connellan, Geoff Dawson, Fred Bayne and Roger Jennings flew to the Gold Coast for the inaugural function.

Millican, a solicitor whose son Anthony lives in Melbourne and has been a (Melbourne) TBC member for the past half-dozen years, said the club often hosted Melbourne-based members who were visiting the Gold Coast for races, sales or holidays.

"We have Melbourne members drop in all the time — especially if Collingwood is playing!

"We have 40 members, and, like Melbourne, it is a terrific group of like-minded racing people who enjoy a good time."

Millican has owned many gallopers down the decades but said "none of them was much good."

"I've had horses with the late Bruce McLauchlan, Alan Bailey and Bevan Laming, who is a member of our Thoroughbred Club.

"I'm not into gardening or golf so I just dedicate my leisure time to the Thoroughbred Club and look forward every year to head to Melbourne for the great Caulfield Cup eve luncheon," he said.

PETER STUBBS used the Thoroughbred Club as the blueprint to establish a social outlet for the Canberra Racing Club.

Stubbs, who is on the cusp of retirement after 30 years in racing administration including a stint as chief executive in Albury, has been an innovator during his 12 years as chief executive of the CRC.

Among his achievements are the completion of the $13.5 million capital works for training facilities, an increase of 70 per cent in prizemoney levels, the elimination of debt and the merging of the club's premier event, the Black Opal Stakes and Canberra Cup with the Opal upgraded to Group 3 level.

However, Stubbs wanted more for racing folk — including himself when he retires — and three years ago he instigated the Thoroughbred Club as the Canberra Racing Club's social arm.

"I'd been to Melbourne for the Caulfield Cup eve function and I recognised the Thoroughbred Club as the ideal type of gathering I wanted for Canberra," he said. "I spoke to Roger (Jennings) about it and he was really helpful and greatly supportive.

"We are still developing but we have 100 members on the list and when we have a big function such as the Black Opal Stakes function (on the Friday before the Sunday running of the club's main event) we have 120+ people, which for a young club in a small zone is a good start.

> "We have a mix of people who simply are interested in racing and having some fun"

"We have a mix of people, just like Melbourne, with owners and breeders and trainers and people who simply are interested in racing and having some fun.

"One of our meetings involved two guest speakers: Michael Thomas who owns Happy Clapper and Pat Webster who trains him. Michael is a local and his father Jack is a former president of the Canberra Racing Club.

"We have a good time and as I am retiring soon I want a club to attend where I can enjoy myself among racing people. Our Thoroughbred Club offers that."

THE THOROUGHBRED CLUB has been informed and entertained by an exceptional array of guest speakers.

One of the most unlikely was Captain Mark Phillips. Although he had no official role at the luncheon he responded to his welcome to the function by relating his racing interests and wide involvement with equestrian events.

Another was Ron Walker, then the Lord Mayor of Melbourne, who spoke on innumerable topics while presenting the trophy to the winning owners of the 1973 Caulfield Cup, Swell Time.

Walker, who died in January of 2018, was the Lord Mayor of Melbourne from 1974 to 1976 but is recognised more in business and for his work in managing sporting events.

He became chairman of the Australian Grand Prix Corporation after he delivered Melbourne the hosting rights from Adelaide to host the event in 1993.

He was appointed chairman of the Melbourne Major Events Company, the body which managed both the bids for the Grand Prix and the 2006 Commonwealth Games. Walker was also the Chairman of Melbourne 2006, the organising body for the 2006 Commonwealth Games.

During his business career he held large stakes in companies such as People Telecom, Primelife and Buka Minerals.

In 1976, he and Lloyd Williams formed a property development company, Hudson Conway, which developed the Crown Casino complex in Melbourne and was the casino's first operator, and resigned from the group in 2000.

Walker also served as Chairman of the Microsurgery Foundation of the Bernard O'Brien Institute and was renowned for his collection of classic cars and property.

SIR ZELMAN COWEN was another guest speaker of the highest quality, an Australian legal scholar and university administrator who served as the 19th Governor-General of Australia.

He addressed members in August of 1997, giving a detailed account of Governor Generals of Australia and his own appointment and experiences.

Born in Melbourne and educated at Scotch College and the University of Melbourne, Cowen served in the Royal Australian Navy before attending New College, Oxford, on a Rhodes Scholarship and winning the prestigious Vinerian Scholarship as the best student in the Bachelor of Civil Law degree.

In 1951, Cowen returned to Australia to become dean of the law faculty at the University of Melbourne. He later served as vice-chancellor of the University of New England (1966–1970) and the University of Queensland (1970–1977).

In 1977, Prime Minister Malcolm Fraser appointed Cowen to succeed John Kerr as governor-general. He was an uncontroversial choice, and became the second Jewish holder of the position, after Sir Isaac Isaacs. After leaving office, Cowen returned to academia, serving as provost of Oriel College, Oxford, from 1982 to 1990.

"The Thoroughbred Club has enjoyed nobody of higher recognition"

After his retirement he returned to Australia and became active in Jewish community affairs in Melbourne. He also pursued a range of other interests, including serving for five years on the board of Fairfax Newspapers (three of them as Chairman) during a turbulent period for the company; and being patron of St Kilda Football Club.

Cowen, who died in December of 2011, at the age of 92, was given a state funeral in Melbourne which was attended by the Governor-General, Dame Quentin Bryce, the Prime Minister, Julia Gillard, the Opposition Leader, Tony Abbott, and former Prime Ministers Malcolm Fraser, Bob Hawke and John Howard.

The Thoroughbred Club has enjoyed nobody of higher recognition. His first honour was a Knight Bachelor in 1976. When appointed Governor-General he was made a Knight Grand Cross of the Order of St Michael and St George (GCMG) and Knight of the Order of Australia (AK) in 1977, and sworn of the Privy Council in 1977. When Queen Elizabeth visited Australia in 1980 she appointed Cowen a Knight Grand Cross of the Royal Victorian Order (GCVO).

ONE of the most unusual and informative gatherings occurred at the 1995 Caulfield Cup eve luncheon, which celebrated the 50th anniversary of the 1945 Cup when St Fairy defeated Rainbird and Punctilia.

The jockeys of the place getters, Scobie Breasley (St Fairy), Ron Hutchinson (Rainbird) and Jack Purtell (Punctilia) were special guests. Bill Collins interviewed the three legendary jockeys — all four of them members of Racing's Hall of Fame — as they relived the great race and related a wide range of riding stories.

Bill Collins MC'd almost all Caulfield Cup Eve luncheons under Harry Harrison's chairmanship until he passed on in 1997. Ron Casey took over for a couple of years before he too died in 2000. Gary Gray took the microphone for a couple of years before Craig Willis became the permanent MC, with Tony Leonard standing in when Craig was unavailable.

BILL COLLINS was one of many media personalities who entertained the Thoroughbred Club as guest speaker. In September of 1984 he reviewed international racing in Japan, England, Ireland and Barbados, along with their betting facilities, after a recent trip.

Lou Richards put on a show in 1977, while the following year *The Truth*'s racing editor Ron Taylor, who celebrated his 90th birthday in May of 2018, spoke informatively about the timing of major spring race days and the re-arrangement of lead up races, along with the problems associated with the clashes with other codes.

ABC race caller Joe Brown spoke with authority and passion about the history of race calling and well-known identities involved in that difficult profession, while, also in 1981, John Russell discussed his recent racing tour of the US that took in the American Triple Crown, the attraction that draws crowds of 130,000-plus, horse farms/studs of Kentucky and comparisons with Australian racing.

Brown returned 19 years later after his retirement, taking a nostalgic look at race broadcasters he had known and the unfortunate rationalisation of racing radio stations.

In June of 1982, the Editor of the *Weekly Times*, John Balfour-Brown, recalled his involvement with racing as a jumps rider and trainer, point to point, polo and equestrian events. He was generations ahead of his time when he covered issues relative to the RSPCA, the animal liberation movement and problems with jumping in the eyes of the public.

A few months later, Flemington clocker Des Spain informed the TBC on racing issues, racing writers and trackmen operations, while in November Leon Weigard delivering an enlightening and humorous account of his involvement with sports, concentrating on football (he was president of Fitzroy), water polo (he was an Olympian) and racing.

Radio and TV personality John McMahon recounted his life's involvement over 40 years in radio as Breakfast Announcer, Toastmaster to the City of Melbourne, MC of *Radio Talent Time* and his involvement in boxing and racing.

Later in 1984 Jack Strying, a *Herald and Weekly Times* racing journalist and race caller, enlightened members on reasons behind diminishing attendances at metropolitan race meetings and the escalating costs of thoroughbreds. Styring also talked on the failure of race club administrators to adequately market Thoroughbred Racing by instead relying on the self-supporting position of yesteryear of funding racing through the turnstiles. Styring, who called 47 Gunbower Cups, also spoke in March of 1991 and 1998 and April of 2003, never failing to entertain.

Also, in 1984 Bob Bottoms, journalist and author, gave an extensive recount of the "Age Tapes", an account of his time as advisor to the NSW Government on organised crime which covered race fixing to drug trafficking, and questionable racing administrators in NSW to the involvement of Robert Trimboli and George Freeman.

In August of 1985, the nation's most influential racing journalist, Jack Elliott, gave an enlightening account of the highlights of his racing career from 1938 which took in several English Derbys, comparations in International Racing and Breeding, and his views on the greatest riders he had seen and the greatest racehorse, Tulloch.

The following month Murray Bell, the Australian editor of *Bloodhorse Magazine*, spoke on Professionalism and International standards in Thoroughbred Breeding and the lack of attention that is paid to detail and publicise Australian thoroughbreds.

Far more controversial early the following year was Keith Hillier, Chief racing writer of *The Sun*, who gave an in-depth account of his views that Melbourne had been dethroned by Sydney as the Racing Capital of Australia — from breeding, racing, training and marketing. He returned in September of 2008 to reflect on his earlier comments.

In March of 1987 Bryan Martin, the 3DB race caller and director of Raceplay, outlined his 15 years calling races, the problems facing race broadcasting, and Raceplay's role in marketing various leading sporting identities.

The following year, one of Melbourne most respected and controversial journalists, Tom Prior of *The Sun*, gave an account of interviewing and reporting methods and techniques, and unusual experiences over his many years as specialist reporter. He was a witness to the last hanging in Australia, Ronald Ryan, and covered most of the major crime and sports stories over four decades.

In the same year, the legendary Ron Casey covered the past couple of decades of his involvement with the Olympics and media coverage. He returned as guest speaker three years later to give members a detailed account of Melbourne's bid for the 1996 Olympics, the reason why it had become money driven and what Los Angeles did to turn the Games around to a highly profitable exercise. He explained the bid budget was $19 million – 50% funded by company sponsorship with the balance funded by State and Local Government. He suggested prospects were strong.

In September that year, the club held its first convened formal monthly meeting at night to coincide and support the OIC announcement of the 1996 Olympics and Melbourne's bid, which, unfortunately, was unsuccessful.

Despite the disappointment of missing out on the Olympics, Casey ploughed on with other issues. As chairman of North Melbourne Football Club, he returned in September of 1996 to give an in-depth account of current AFL merger activities, their shortcomings and the future direction of the League's expansion plans.

The Thoroughbred Club broke new ground in September of 1988 when ABC television presenter Mary Delahunty became the first female to attend a monthly meeting and address members as guest speaker. She enlightened members on her introduction to reporting, different experiences — and difficult ones — on the theme of making one's own luck.

In November of 1988, then Channel Ten sportscaster/editor Bruce McAvaney gave his usual highly-polished presentation and account of the Seoul 1988 Olympic movement.

The following year, *Sunday Observer* chief sports sub-editor Peter Hendy recounted many years of activity and changes in getting sports results to press, and some lighter moments of well-known racing journalists.

He was followed in November that year by the incomparable journalist Les Carlyon, who gave members an account of racing industry changes over the past eight years, and the concentration in top-of-the-market yearling sales inflated and driven by tax domination.

One Australia's, most respected cricket and football identities, Bill Jacobs, related his amazing experiences and highlights as a cricketer (captain of Fitzroy), Australian cricket team manager and lifetime as a football and cricket broadcaster in November of 1990.

In April of 1995, John Darcy — a MVRC/VRC committeeman, director of Racing Victoria and former chairman of the *Herald and Weekly Times* — provided members with a knowledgeable insight into Cable-Pay TV and the players involved, aspects of the three-Party Licenses and its effects on free-to-air TV, Sky TV and racing.

In September of 1997, *Herald Sun* sports writer Jon Anderson recounted his introduction to racing at an early age and his many highlights of racing and great horses, while three years later former *Herald* racing writer Rhett Kirkwood spoke about his book on Phar Lap.

An interesting speaker in 2001 was Graeme Alford, author and promoter, who outlined his life from scholastic achievements, his wayward course through law to conviction for armed robbery and time spent in Pentridge. He told of how he turned his life around and his success in bringing together the "World Masters of Business" by luring to Australia General Schmarskopt, Lee Iaccoca, Mikhail Gorbachev and Nelson Mandela.

Television personality and author John Harms stepped up in March of 2008 while in August journalist Andre Kassay, who went on to join the stewards' panel as a form guide guru, spoke of his experiences, as did *Millers Guide* owner Dennis Huxley in November of 2009.

In June of 2012, Michael Harms, a man whose experience included roles as the Executive Chairman of RSN racing and sport radio station, a partner and business director at national marketing agency George Patterson Partners and managing director of Channel Seven Melbourne, provided great insight into media and racing. Rod Nicholson returned to the Melbourne Cricket Ground in April of 2014 to relate his experiences as News Limited's international cricket correspondent over 23 years and his involvement over 48 years in the racing game, while a year later David Mann, the promotions manager of 3AW, gave his views on racing and radio and promotions.

Greg Miles graced the club and reminisced about his record 36 Melbourne and Caulfield Cup calls, while a year later radio personality and singer/composer Greg Champion entertained the members. And to kick off 2018, "Dr Turf" John Rothfield told a tale or two about his role in the media and racing.

ALONG with the entertainment came a wealth of experience and knowledge from racing administrators, officials, breeders and others who contribute to the industry, always keeping members abreast of the latest developments.

In 1970 the TAB's general manager Jack Rutter explained the complications and bonuses of the introduction of the Rimfire System, which revolutionised wagering in Victoria.

Club member Mark Read provided members with inside information about punting, as well as breeding that helped him enjoy a dominance on the national racing landscape, while also in 1979, Bill Stutt provided an illuminating, nostalgic reflection of a lifetime in racing.

Racing's chief steward of the day, Pat Lalor (now a long-standing club member) gave a complete rundown of the work of stewards in February of 1981, explaining roles involving nominations, inspection of horses, barrier draws and swabbing, as well as an outline of how stewards determine protests and how protests can affect race results.

Lalor returned two years later to give members a full and comprehensive account of the new Racing Appeals Tribunal, its structure and how it will serve all racing codes in Victoria. He also questioned the value of the Government Committee being formed to control racing.

Showing great foresight in 1981 was club member Keith Jones, the headmaster of Mentone Grammar, who gave a presentation on topical industry racing matters, the need for a singular racing body, all-weather tracks, and the re-framing and re-programming of classic races.

Other informative speakers that year Sir Rupert Steele who concentrated on the escalating prices of yearlings, the development of racing in Victoria compared with New South Wales, and the apparent lack of promotion and confidence in the Victorian Thoroughbred Industry, and Bobby Rackard, the manager elect of Nelson Bunker-Hunt Thoroughbred Stud on his experiences on the international breeding scene and, in particular, the Irish National Stud on its breeding methods, housing mares and affiliated services.

Also educating club members that year was Brian Maher of Thoroughbred International, who flew in from Queensland for the meeting. He spoke on his involvement in breeding and the substantial capital gains available from thoroughbred breeding, as well as his multi-million-dollar disbursal sale in Queensland.

At the start of 1982, Graham Campbell, the Australian manager of Dalgety's Bloodstock, spoke on the international breeding and racing scene, forced values on yearling thoroughbreds overseas and comparisons of racing worldwide. He returned the following year to defend the $5 million purchase of the Dalgety's Oaklands Junction Sales Complex, as well as expressing the need for the barrier between breeders and promoters to be broken down.

Upon his retirement two years later, Campbell spoke openly on the essentials of commercial thoroughbred breeding and shortcomings in Victoria compared with NSW for a failure to properly promote stallions and ensure quality broodmares. He suggested that, contrary to previous results, poorer quality yearlings were bringing high prices, but he expected that to change.

He was followed by Judge Bill Martin who spoke of his many years in racing, highlighted by his involvement with racing appeals and the many identities involved.

VRC committeeman and principal of Stockwell Stud Farm, Ken Cox, chimed in with discussions about racing administration and the breeding industry. He returned several months later to give his take on racing administration, the Thoroughbred Breeders Association, his TAB involvement and the Government's drag on racing. He also covered his involvement as Chairman of the Taxation Appeals Board and the lack of support to deal with relief in all areas of the Thoroughbred Industry.

Sports Minister Neil Trezise covered controversial moves since coming to power — after race payouts, an appeals tribunal, funds distribution to the codes and 3DB's contract handed out to cover all codes including interstate race broadcasts.

Another foresighted speaker was Brendan McCarthy (pre-club membership) in early 1983.

The President of Bloodhorse Breeders Association of Victoria gave a highly informative account of the BBA movement and the industry problems. He accounted for statistical information and industry losses of more than $20 million between 1981 and 1983.

He also touched on Victoria's problems with fashionable sires standing interstate and proposed a BBA incentive scheme with premiums to all Victorian races for two-year-olds, spreading to three and four-year-olds, to be provided to owners of brood mares, stallion owners, trainers, jockeys and registered owners.

Terry Minchan, in company with John Augustine of London Bloodstock Insurance, detailed that only three in 100 thoroughbreds accounted for claims.

Minchan also gave an account of devastating Epsom Derby winner Shergar's horse napping from the Aga Khan's Stud. Shergar was booked for Stud Service at 50,000 pounds and had an estimated value of 15 million pounds against an Insurance payout of 6.5 million pounds. Shergar was abducted and never found.

Retired VRC handicapper Kevin Ryan addressed the club in August of 1984 and returned in February of 1987 to update members on Australian racing, the concept of one-club multi racecourse principal city operations, attendance problems and the standard of growing sponsorship.

In November of 1985 Rod Johnson, then then VRC Racing Manager, recounted changes to Thoroughbred racing over his 30-plus years covering the introduction of the photo finish, starting stalls, stewards patrol films, swabbing, pre-race blood testing and the advent of the TAB and sponsorship. He also gave an account of some of the lighter moments of the inner sanctum of VRC Committee Meetings in his inimitable style. He returned as VRC secretary in September of 1986 and gave a full insight into the administrative structure of Victoria's premier race club. Upon his retirement as VRC chief executive/ secretary, he spoke again in November of 1995.

Another intriguing address came in March of 1985 when Jack Rutter, the retired General Manager of the TAB, covered the establishment of the TAB in March 1981, it's growth, direction and difficulties encountered with Government intervention, and the changing effect on the racing side of operations.

Club member Graeme Sampieri, the highly-regarded bookmaker and commission agent, spoke in April of 1985 about his 20 years of bookmaking from small Saturday country meetings to the races on all leading metropolitan tracks. He lamented the decrease in bookmaker numbers from 1500 to 500 and the fall in percentages from 25% to 7% and predicted a dismal future for bookies. He also covered some humorous accounts of doing battle with the punters over the years. He returned 13 years later to emphasise his belief that bookmakers were an endangered species.

Later in 1985 Geoff Hazard, the veterinary surgeon to the VRC and MVRC, presented slides and gave members an extensive insight into the problems breeders encounter with birth defects in new thoroughbred foals, and appropriate remedial actions.

Also imparting knowledge was club member Nick Column, who spoke of his interest in racing and breeding, his failures and successes, culminating in his purchase of Magari and Tristarc as a yearling, the latter going on to win that year's (1985) Caulfield Cup.

The following year Murray Achilles, the Australian manager of Wrightson Bloodstock, gave an account of his 28 years with Wright Stephenson, the New Zealand reliance on the Australian Bloodstock Industry and the Patrick Hogan/ Sir Tristram story and what it had done for the New Zealand Bloodstock Industry. Murray joined the Club in 1986 and resigned from the Club following his retirement in 1993 when he retired to the Western District. Sadly, not that long after, he and his wife lost their lives in a rail crossing accident when leaving their retirement property.

Another bloodstock agent, Richard Galpin of the Newmarket (UK) Bloodstock Agency, provided members with informative comparisons of Australian racing and breeding with the major countries of Great Britain and America as well as stipulating the strengths and benefits of Australian racing.

In August of 1986, John Messara, the chairman of ARABS, member of the Sydney Stock Exchange and amongst other things, Federal Treasurer of the Bloodhorse Breeders Association, fly down from Sydney to address the meeting. He outlined the problems the Australian thoroughbred confronted compared with its overseas counterpart, the lack of genuine cooperation between states and other horse racing bodies and authorities which were affecting the progress of the industry.

Messara also gave members an insight into Public Company roles here and in New Zealand in breeding and racing.

Phillip Power, the Director of Racing and Gaming, Sport and Recreation, spoke in 1987 about the concept of the Tabaret, and the purchase of Radio Station 3UZ by racing bodies, having been part of the working body to acquire it what is now Radio Sports National (RSN) 927.

Then Shadow Minister for Sport, Tom Reynolds, spoke in 1989 about the state government's grab of TAB income previously earmarked for distribution to race clubs, and promised (and delivered) the return of unclaimed dividends to racing when he took over as Liberal Sports Minister.

That same year, Peter Williams, the assistant to the Secretary of the VRC, enlightened members on the proposals and lead-up to placing all restricted races on a uniform national basis from December of 1989. He was part of the steering Committee.

Another insightful talk came early the following year from Graham Brooke, a consultant who led the VRC and Country Racing Council study into training facilities in Victoria. He discussed his findings and the demands and requirements of training establishments.

What's in a name? Well, Eric Jeffrey, the VRC Registrar of Racehorses and Ticket Secretary told plenty of tales about that when he retired and spoke in January of 1991. The following month Bill Stutt, recently retired chairman of the MVRC, told of his introduction to the thoroughbred industry and his lifetime involvement with racing.

In September that year, John "Darcy" Duggan gave members an enlightening and humorous account of his many years on the "Bench" as Chief Stipendiary Magistrate, as well as an update on the direction being taken by the Review Board into gambling machines and Casinos.

The following January, Ian McEwen — the retired Chief Executive of the MVRC and Consultant to Tabaret — recalled his 20 years with Moonee Valley, the changes to racing, conflicts and the direction of racing administration today, as well as an informative insight into the introduction of poker machines in Victoria.

A month later, Geoff Davies, Tabaret's Sports Book manager, explained the establishment of Tabaret's Sports Book betting coverage and odds setting, embracing all sports.

In contrast, in May of that year, the President of the Bookmakers Association, Geoff Donald, addressed members on the issues and problems being encountered by all bookmakers operating on racing. He cited the loss of market share or legal gambling dollar over the past 30 years from 90% to 13% today. He also outlined the restrictions that denied bookmakers the opportunity to compete for increased turnover.

The following month Phil Power, the director for racing and gaming, spoke of the issues facing the racing industry with the introduction of gaming machines and the competition for the gambling dollar. He returned in 2000 to give examples of the complexity of the distribution of the gaming dollar and the spread of Internet gaming.

In February of 1992, VATC committee members took club members on a guided tour of the second stage of the Rupert Clarke Stand, while a year later, racehorse syndicator Harry Lawton explained his 20 years involvement in syndication and experiences and highlights in syndicating more than 600 thoroughbreds.

A year later Michael Classon, the Chief Executive of the MVRC told of the challenge when replacing Ian McEwen. He gave his view of the problems facing the Thoroughbred Racing Industry and presented a stewards' tape involving protests, interference and improper riding charges, many of which, in hindsight, were particularly humorous.

Rod Fitzroy, a leading Industry racehorse owner and later chairman of the VRC, that year outlined "VICTRIE", a presentation to the Government of the importance of Thoroughbred Racing to the Victorian economy. Five years late, as a VRC committeeman, he reported on the Emperors Cup in Japan and the VRC presentation and promotion of Racing Victoria and the Melbourne Cup to the Japan Racing Association which eventually led to a Japanese quinella in the Melbourne Cup.

Dr John Bourke, the VRC Senior Veterinary Steward gave members an insight into drug administration, detection and the support role of veterinary science to stewards and to cap off 1993 Les Benton, the VRC Racing Manager, told of quarantine arrangements and training facilities provided to Irish and English gallopers Vintage Crop and Drum Taps for the Melbourne Cup. He returned the following year to update members on overseas entries for the 1994 Melbourne Cup.

The variety of speakers continued in 1994 with Dale Monteith telling of his racing from childhood to the post of VATC chief executive; club member Arthur White entertaining with lighter moments of 45 years of bookmaking, punting and the current problems facing bookmakers. Another club member (international) Bill Bartlett told of his part ownership of the San Houston Race Track in America and drew interesting comparisons between US and Australian racing.

Early in 1995 Mark O'Sullivan — the Chief Executive of the Victorian Country Racing Council, a director of Racing Victoria and a member of the Racing Reform Group, Vision 2000 — outlined issues with the Leadership 2000 business plan and notably the many negatives raised in an article published in *The Age* by Les Carlyon, entitled "Flogging a Dead Horse".

In the first year of the Blue Diamond eve luncheon, in 1995, the general manager of marketing of the Association for the Blind, Ian Wilson, explained the background behind founding of Association and its aims. He extended sincere thanks to all members for supporting the Blue Diamond luncheon.

The following year Leigh Jordan, the secretary/manager of the VOBIS Industry Incentive Scheme since its inception, incorporating the new Super Vobis and Australian Triple Crown, covered the background and development of the highly successful incentive. On the administrative side, members were treated to informative talks from VRC chief executive Brian Beattie, VRC racing manager Les Benton and MVRC chief executive Paul Bretell.

Two racing identities entertained members in 1997. Ian McEwen, the chairman of Harness Racing Victoria and the acclaimed past Chief Executive of Moonee Valley, took members through his involvement in racing in New Zealand and Victoria, his highs and lows and many achievements and experiences.

Then Des Gleeson, recently appointed chairman of stewards, spoke of his background, his cadetship and rise to the top as well as the number of controversial issues arising in his early days at the helm. He returned the following year to report on issues regarding overseas entries at the Spring Carnival and the lift in stakes because of international competition. He also explained the rules applicable to protest hearings given the controversy of recent protest hearings involving International runners.

Politician Vin Heffernan gave an insight into the reigning Liberal Party activities in 1998, including the Kennett operation and his own political career, while Bill Stutt, the former chairman of Moonee Valley, recounted his childhood and teenage years developing an understanding of thoroughbred racing and breeding, including his early days associated with Novelty Pony Races. He also recounted memorable moments, including his association with Tommy Woodcock and the great Phar Lap.

Also that year, the Chief Executive of Sandown Park Greyhounds, John Stephens, spoke on the development of international greyhound racing and the Top Gun Series. He also spoke of the promotion of the Melbourne Cup after his visit to England, Ireland and America. Another politician, Bill McGrath, the Minister for Police and Corrections, as well as Coolmore Australia marketing consultant James Bester and club member Peter Maher (Rehame monitoring) spoke during 1998.

In 1999, members donated $1390 to the Peter Maccallum Cancer Institute after Prof. John Zalcberg gave an informative speech about all cancers but concentrating on prostate cancer.

One of the nice guys in the backroom of racing, Ron King, told of his almost half-century as general manager of operations at the VRC and recounted his many years associated with thoroughbreds and track administration, as well as Flemington's controversial straight six.

Club member Paul Leeds gave an important talk in 2000 about Sport 927. The chairman of the racing radio station as well as managing director of Leeds Media and Communications, gave an insight into the past, present and future issues facing Sport 927, racing acquisition issues and the pressures being faced to service as much of racing industry as possible while keeping a balance with commercial radio requirements.

One of the more unusual talks came from art entrepreneur Rod Menzies, on the cusp of becoming a club member late in 2000. He took members into the world of art, auctions and some lighter moments of business activities of Menzies International Cleaning Services, as well as his 25 years of thoroughbred racing, breeding and sponsorship involvement.

The roles of apprentices, stablehands and support staff was explored by Racing Victoria's Education and Training Centre's Ron Hall and Juilette Rault, while later in 2000 Les Twentyman, the Youth Outreach Worker with a long and notable history of assisting disadvantaged young people, made an address on social issues confronting youth, drug problems and what everyone can do to assist disadvantaged youth.

In January of 2001, recently retired chairman of stewards, Par Lalor, gave great insight into some of the most famous and controversial protests he had encountered, including the Big Philou Caulfield Cup protest and subsequent Melbourne Cup doping, the 1972 jumps racing enquiry, the Marwong/Our Poetic Prince protest, the Ararat Cup enquiry and the Royal School/Regal Vista ring-in.

Graham Brooke, a former club member, recounted his disgust that he was commissioned by the Principal Racing Clubs in 1990 to report on Racing Clubs, Training Establishments and the use of facilities, only for the report to be shelved without review and never released publicly.

The recently appointed Chief Executive of the Melbourne Racing Club, Peter Sweeney, spoke mainly about his passion for golf, recounting his background from Berrigan in NSW 47 years earlier to his high as Australian Amateur Golf Champion, while early in 2002 Racing Victoria racecourse detective Peter McWilliams told of his interest in racing and his former role as Snr Detective with Victoria Police. He presented members with an insight into the role of Racecourse Detective and its parameters to combat crime and maintain the integrity of the industry.

Victoria's former premier Jeff Kennett, then the president of the Hawthorn Football Club and head of Beyondblue, spoke brilliantly in June of 2007 while VRC chairman Rod Fitzroy took members to Flemington to see first-hand the new mounting yard and stalls.

In 2009 the Melbourne Racing Club's head of racecourses Jason Kerr, Racing Victoria's head steward Terry Bailey and Inglis sales director Simon Vivian, along with trainer Mick Price and jockey Craig Newitt provided a variety of information on different topics.

The following year also provided variety, with Melbourne Racing Club chief executive Alasdair Robertson, bookmakers Graeme Sampieri, Geoff Donald and Peter Seers telling tales of the satchel, former jockey Peter Hutchinson getting plenty of laughs and art expert Rod Menzies illuminating members on priceless pieces.

They were followed up in 2011 by Ron Iddles, a detective from the Homicide Squad, international administrator Mark Player and champion trainer Peter Moody. To boot, members went to Swettenham Stud and Mitchleton Winery for lunch as well as dining at Moonee Valley in a fundraiser for jockey Brett Scott. Next up were Des O'Keefe, the secretary of the Jockeys Association, jockey Craig Williams and his manager Mark Guest, a trip to Parliament House to listen to Racing Minister Dennis Napthine, and another trip to Fowles/Plunketts Restaurant on a visit to Darley Stud.

Members were treated to lunch at Living Legends at Oaklands in 2013, along with talks with Racing Victoria chairman Rob Roulston, chief executive Bernard Saundry and chief vet Brian Stewart. Other guest speakers were Professor Garry Jennings of the Baker IDI Heart & Diabetes Institute, the manager of Betezy Grant Kean and Victoria's Racing Integrity Commissioner Sal Perna.

In 2014, then AFL deputy chief executive Gillon McLaughlin answered many questions at a luncheon at the RACV club, while the general manager of marketing and strategy at RVL, Andrew Catterall, gave an insightful speech. Also that year, MRC honorary treasurer Matt Cain, and club member and trainer Ken Keys provided variety.

Members also were guests of politician Craig Ondarchie in the Parliament House Members Dining Room and enjoyed a visit to Darley Stud to look at the stallions and enjoy lunch.

Champion trainer Darren Weir, on the verge of training Prince Of Penzance to win the 2015 Melbourne Cup, was heartily welcomed at the RACV Club, while other speakers for the year were Chris Burke, the managing director of International Horse Transport, bookmaker and club member Mark Read and the chief executive of Country Racing Victoria, Scott Whiteman. Members also were entertained at club member Anthony Mithen's Rosemont Stud.

One of the highlights of 2016 was a celebration of the horse's birthday in the Parliament House Members Dining Room, where members and guests were addressed by the Shadow Minister for Racing, Tim Bull. Speakers that year were Racing Victoria's General Manager of Racing, Greg Carpenter, trainer Robbie Griffiths, French trainer John Fellows and RVL's horse racing consultant Paul Bittar. Another tour of Swettenham Stud and lunch at Mitchelton Winery capped off the year.

To end the first 50 years of the club, the 2017 year provided speeches from Racing.com chief executive Andrew Catterall, retired chief steward and director of TAS racing, Des Gleeson, trainer Troy Corstens, and Rod Nicholson interviewing trainer Darren Weir and chief steward Terry Bailey. Trainer David Hayes gave members an insightful look at his Lindsay Park Racing stables at Euroa.

THROUGHOUT the first 50 years of the Thoroughbred Club, a diverse array of talent has informed and entertained members. While always trying to include racing on the agenda, organisers also looked for engaging speakers.

Champion jockey Roy Higgins addressed members in 1974 and 1978, reflecting on his illustrious career. "The Professor" rode 108 Group 1 winners among 247 metropolitan stakes wins. He won the Victorian jockeys premiership 11 times and rode some of the champions of the era. He rode 2312 winners including two Melbourne Cups (Light Fingers in 1965 and Red Handed in 1967), a Caulfield Cup on Big Philou in 1969, a Cox Plate on Gunsynd in 1972, four Victoria Derbys, five VRC Oaks and four Blue Diamond Stakes.

In 1980, Bill Collins diverged from his usual racing chat to enlighten members of sport in Russia, the Moscow Olympics which he broadcast, and racing/trotting at the Moscow Hippodrome. The following year Father John Brosnan, fittingly on St Patricks Day, spoke about his social work, sports activities and many of his associations over his lifetime.

Many others — including ALP boss Clyde Holding, Melbourne Lord Mayor Ted Best, chairman of stewards Jim Ahern and leading veterinarian Dr John Bourke — generously gave their time to help club members enjoy monthly meetings.

But it was not all about racing.

In 1987, legendary Hawthorn footballer Leigh Matthews gave a detailed account of the ups and downs of his career, along with his interests in racing as syndicate head of the "Glenferrie" syndicate.

The same year, the executive commissioner of the Victorian Football League, Allan Schwab, took members through the mechanics of running the VFL, and his involvement and past association with league clubs, Richmond and St Kilda.

In 1988, Vic Rail, the trainer of champion galloper Vo Rogue — accompanied by the *60 Minutes* News Team, gave a humorous account of his controversial training and handling ways, including an account of his association with the Thoroughbred Industry since a 12-year-old and times spent with Tommy Woodcock, the strapper of Phar Lap.

That same year Peter Boyle, the president of the Small Business Association, spoke of his career highlights, parliamentary involvement and trade union movement, while early the following year Brian Pearce took members into the world of art, from collecting to investment.

And what of Ken Page, who gave members the inside story on having an entrant in ocean racing and the Admiral's Cup?

Or brilliant television personality and broadcaster Tony Charlton, better known for his sport, who spoke of the meaning of ANZAC, Gallipoli and those thousands who gave their lives for this country?

Champion jockey Ron Hutchinson returned from the UK and spoke of his early days, trainers and people for whom he rode — including the Queen Mother — while Bob Shearer spoke on all things golf, local and International. Club member Noel McMahon told plenty of tales about his years with Melbourne, his career highlights and growing up with racing industry people and racing's ups and downs.

Club members rallied with a donation of $2000 to the Fitzroy Football Club after its president Leon Wiegard spoke in April of 1991 about the eventually futile fight for survival.

The secretary/general manager of the Melbourne Cricket Club, Dr John Lill, advised members on the progress of rebuilding the southern stand, playing surfaces and many interesting issues associated with touring test cricket teams.

Then former champion tennis player and coach Neale Fraser gave an insight into Davis Cup preparation and results over his years as captain, some highlights of his playing years and the antics of high ranking professionals.

In the world of football, the AFL national umpires' director Bill Deller presented members with a "Judge for Yourself" video of controversial umpiring decisions and an enlightening account of years of active umpiring late in 1992. He returned in September of 1995 to answer questions about current umpiring controversies.

Jockey Peter Hutchinson entertained with tall tales concerning his sporting activities and highlights of his riding career, while Simon O'Donnell related his personal sporting accomplishments and many humorous experiences on the international cricket circuit.

August of 1994 was an unusual meeting — club president Henry Harrison was absent! Honorary secretary Ian Scroggie chaired the meeting because Harrison was interstate. The only other meeting he had missed in 21 years as president was when he first had open heart surgery!

The guest speaker that day was champion trainer Lee Freedman who spoke of his introduction to racing, commencing as an owner/trainer and developments that lead him to setting up operations in Melbourne.

Also in 1996 Essendon Football Club coach Kevin Sheedy recounted his time from Prahran to Richmond to the rebuilding of Essendon to the ongoing force in the AFL.

Genuine character Brian Mayfield Smith was an enthralling speaker in 1997. He told of his early days until the time he ended the great Tommy Smith's 33 consecutive Sydney trainer premiership record, and of his venture to live in Africa to save native animals.

One of football's great characters, umpire Glenn James, related in 1998 and again in 2005 many humorous yarns from his career, pointing out that being Aborigine did have its drawbacks in the early days.

In 1999, club member John Sutcliffe told of the highlights and humorous moments of his umpiring career with the VFL, while later that year AFL executive Ron Joseph, entertained with yarns of his days at North Melbourne, at the VFL with Alan Aylett and Jack Hamilton and his present duties at the AFL Commission.

Peter Carey, the AFL and All-Australian umpire related some controversial, some compromising and some confusing experiences throughout his career, highlighted by his remarkable "marking" effort during an AFL match.

Tennis was the topic in late 2001 when champion Frank Sedgman and Australian Davis Cup senior selector and former champion Allan Stone regaled the members. Sedgman drew comparisons to his US Open win 50 years ago and Leighton Hewitt in 2001 — the major difference being Hewitt's $1.8m compared to his $25 in money orders. The pair exchanged thoughts on earlier days; Frank under coach Harry Hopman and Allan on some of his finer junior days.

Then it was athletics with Chris Wardlaw, the dual Olympian and Head Coach of the 2000 Olympics Australian Track and Field squad, talking his way through a century of significant Olympic moments leading up to Cathy Freeman's world record 400m run at the 2000 Olympics.

Football was next with Carlton greats Stephen Kernahan and Greg Williams (in an interview with club PR Ian Coutts) going through their careers and some on-and-off field highlights. They also compared modern day football with their era.

Retired jockey Gary Willetts waltzed down memory lane in 2002, reflecting on the 1960s to 1980s when he crossed from New Zealand, the highlights of his career and some outstanding racehorses and associations he has experienced.

One of the great stories of the time was the remarkable survival and recuperation of North Melbourne footballer Jason McCartney. He told his story to members in November of 2006 of his horrific injuries sustained in the Bali bombing and his subsequent return to the playing arena.

Test cricketer Rodney Hogg provided his funny stories in September of 2007 and a couple of months later trainer John Sadler gave an insight into the ups and downs of his training career.

The following year former Melbourne champion and media personality Gary Lyon took the stage, followed some months later, appropriately at Brew House, by Geelong champ and media personality Billy Brownless.

Champion jockey Ron Hutchinson, a club member and Australian Racing Hall of Fame inductee, chatted about his career in 2009, as did prominent trainer Mark Kavanagh who was on a roll with Whobegotyou winning the 2008 Caulfield Guineas, Maldivian winning the 2008 Cox Plate and Shocking winning the 2009 Melbourne Cup.

Many other guest speakers have given their time to entertain and educate club members during the first 50 years of our history and their experience and forthright opinions have been a bonus that money cannot buy.

DENISE RYAN has been an integral part of the Thoroughbred Club for 25 years and arguably gets to see more members at any given function than anyone.

Denise has managed the club's functions since the TBC moved functions to the Caulfield racecourse and has become a personal friend of many prominent members. "I actually knew (Melbourne Racing Club committeeman) Ian Macdonald's parents and I started as a waitress at the Sandown greyhounds where I got to know Henry Harrison and Geoff Dawson.

"I have made a lot of friends. I was invited to Geoff and Loretta Dawson's 40th wedding anniversary and I was always invited to the Thoroughbred Club's Christmas parties as a guest.

> "There was no drama and sure enough, Santa would land on the racetrack"

"I remember one of the funny things that happened every year at the Christmas party at Caulfield. The Melbourne Racing Club would tell me every year to make sure that the helicopter that delivered Father Christmas didn't land on the track.

"And every year the committee would inform me that there was no drama and sure enough, Santa would land on the racetrack. Even though many members of the MRC committee were in attendance, nothing was ever said," she said. Denise said it was sad to lose so many old timers over the years but that they were replaced by other wonderful characters.

"I worked with all the presidents from Henry Harrison's day, and the presidents and the committee and long-time members treat me like an honoured guest, rather than the function manager.

"That goes for so many members, too. I retired six years ago but the MRC kept me on as a casual so that I could continue to manage the Thoroughbred Club functions. I probably look forward to each function as much as, if not more than, the members themselves.

THE first 50 years of the Thoroughbred Club has provided members with a running commentary of the racing industry. Think of the Melbourne Cup experiences, from the first of a running double by Rain Lover in the inaugural year of 1968 and involving the doping of Cup favourite Big Philou, to the initial international success by Vintage Crop to Makybe Diva's unprecedented hat-trick, to Michelle Payne's achievement as the first female jockey to salute, to the reward for effort for Lloyd Williams with five Cup winners.

Think too of the changes to the industry, to which Club members have been privy to explanation by the code's inner sanctum: the development of the TAB, the creation of Racing Victoria, the introduction of corporate bookmakers, of boutique racing television via TVN and now Racing.com, and of night racing.

We have been entertained by some of the legends of racing, many of whom are no longer among us: Bart Cummings, Scobie Breasley, Roy Higgins, Bill Collins and Ron Casey among them.

The Thoroughbred Club has built a legacy. From humble beginnings it has attracted some of the most powerful and influential people in racing, be they breeders, owners, administrators, bookmakers and general horse-loving folk.

Those who have been involved during the past half-century have influenced the fabric of racing in this state. Their dedication and foresight has been instrumental in developments in all areas, and fortunately they have enjoyed an intelligent sounding board within the corridors of the club.

Members have been entertained royally through the decades. They have attended quality establishments, eaten and sipped the best quality, mingled with like-minded racing people and listened to some amazing tales, tall and true.

They have fulfilled one of the mandates of the club — to have fun!

And they have made every effort to ensure another generation of fun-loving, horse-loving people enjoys the same excitement and friendship by instigating The Colts to carry on the club's legacy.

Hopefully this book will help them appreciate those who preceded them, better understand the magnitude of the club's reach and influence, and steel them for a lot of fun and frivolity.

MEMBERS

Tom Curnow
Robin Daley
Darren Dance
Geoff Dawson
Kane Devitt
Peter Devitt
JohnDillon
Roger Donazzan
Domenic D'Ortenzio
Graham Duff
Craig Dunn
Amanda Elliott
Scott Emery
Alistair Ewart
Peter Fekete
JohnFinning
Aaron Fisher
Cameron Fisher
John Ford
Richard Ford
Tom Frazer
Fr. Joe Giacobbe
Mick Gibilisco
Neville Gibson
Martin Godby
Craig Gordon
Russell Gordon
Neil Grant
Alan Green
Robbie Griffiths
Teddy Grimthorpe
Kevin Halpin
Robert Harding
Nick Hassett
Danny Heffernan
Arthur Heintz
Anthony Hodges
Shane Holland
Peter Holmes
Peter Howell
Justin Hoy
Dean Humphries
Pat Hutchinson
Ron Hutchinson
John Hutson
Ross Inglis
Roger Jennings
Tim Johnson
Andre Kassay
Levi Kavanagh
Des Kelly
John Kennedy
Ken Keys
Jason Kidger
Paul King
Adam Kirkwood-Scott
Peter Kopke
Mike Kostos
Merrell Kruger
Griffin Kruger
Jeff Kruger
Pat Lalor
Jamie Lanyon
Ross Lanyon
Laurie Larmer
Peter Lawrence
Gary Lechte
Jon Lechte
Paul Leeds
Paul Lewis
Ian MacDonald
Lachlan MacDonald
David MacLean
John MacLean
Andrew Makiv
Greg Mance
David Mann
Dennis Marks
Len Marks
Paul Martell
Peter Mason
Sam Matthews
Simon McCarthy
Ed McKeon
Noel McMahen
Kane McMonigle
Cameron Menzies

MEMBERS

Michael Alexeeff
Richard Anderson
Robert Anderson
Peter Angus
Terry Bailey
Daniel Barrett
Fraser Bayne
Fred Bayne
Mario Biasin
Joshua Blanksby
Chris Blomeley
Barry Bourke
Keith Brown
Warran Brown
Patrick Browne
Matthew Cain
Peter Caluzzi
Phillip Campbell
Don Casboult
Bill Casimaty
Tony Cavanagh
Robert Christie
Carmine Ciurleo
Bruce Clark
Tony Clifford
Daniel Clohesy
Ken Coles
John Connellan
Jason Cornell
Phillip Cramer
Tom Curnow
Robin Daley
Darren Dance
Geoff Dawson
Kane Devitt
Peter Devitt
John Dillon
Roger Donazzan
Domenic D'Ortenzio
Graham Duff
Craig Dunn
Amanda Elliott
Scott Emery
Alistair Ewart
Peter Fekete
John Finning
Aaron Fisher
Cameron Fisher
John Ford
Richard Ford
Tom Frazer
Fr. Joe Giacobbe
Mick Gibilisco
Neville Gibson
Martin Godby
Craig Gordon
Russell Gordon
Neil Grant
Alan Green
Robbie Griffiths
Teddy Grimthorpe
Kevin Halpin
Robert Harding
Nick Hassett
Danny Heffernan
Arthur Heintz
Anthony Hodges
Shane Holland
Peter Holmes
Peter Howell
Justin Hoy
Dean Humphries
Pat Hutchinson
Ron Hutchinson
John Hutson
Ross Inglis
Roger Jennings
Tim Johnson
Andre Kassay
Levi Kavanagh
Des Kelly
John Kennedy
Ken Keys
Jason Kidger
Paul King
Adam Kirkwood-Scott
Peter Kopke
Mike Kostos
Merrell Kruger
Griffin Kruger
Jeff Kruger
Pat Lalor
Jamie Lanyon
Ross Lanyon
Laurie Larmer
Peter Lawrence

Gary Lechte
Jon Lechte
Paul Leeds
Paul Lewis
Ian MacDonald
Lachlan MacDonald
David MacLean
John MacLean
Andrew Makiv
Greg Mance
David Mann
Dennis Marks
Len Marks
Paul Martell
Peter Mason
Sam Matthews
Simon McCarthy
Ed McKeon
Noel McMahen
Kane McMonigle
Cameron Menzies
Rod Menzies
Alfred Micallef
Anthony Millican
Anthony Mithen
Kevin Munro
Johnathan Munz
Tony Murphy
Peter Murray
Jack Newton
Rod Nicholson
Neil Oates
James O'Brien
Kevin O'Brien
Tim O'Brien
Harvey O'Neill
Benjamin O'Shea
Dallas Patterson
Chris Payne
Craig Pearce
John Phillips
Mark Pilkington
Andrew Pinder
Norm Pinder
John Playfoot
Barry Poynter
Robert Preston
John Radley
Alexander Read
Mark Read
Nicholas Read
Xavier Read
Peter Rossdale
Robert Roulston
John Russell
Graeme Sampieri
Mark Sampieri
Adam Sangster
Bernard Saundry
Ian Scroggie
Peter Seers
Todd Shelton
Michael Sholly
Garry Sidwell
Rob Slade
Les Smith
Michael Smith
Brad Spicer
John Stewart
George Sturesteps
John Sutcliffe
Michael Symons
Ross Teitzel
Brock Thompson
Adam Tims
Michael Tong
Geoff Tucker
Larry Tyler
Peter Vogl
Mark Walkley
David Wallace
Michael Walton
Ken Ward
Scott Whiteman
Glenn Whittenbury
Tim Wildash
Max Williams
Craig Willis
Peter Wilson
Doug Wright
Alan Young

Rod Menzies
Alfred Micallef
Anthony Millican
Anthony Mithen
Kevin Munro
Johnathan Munz
Tony Murphy
Peter Murray
Jack Newton
Rod Nicholson
Neil Oates
James O'Brien
Kevin O'Brien
Tim O'Brien
Harvey O'Neill
Benjamin O'Shea
Dallas Patterson
Chris Payne
Craig Pearce
John Phillips
Mark Pilkington
Andrew Pinder
Norm Pinder
John Playfoot
Barry Poynter
Robert Preston
John Radley
Alexander Read
Mark Read
Nicholas Read
Xavier Read
Peter Rossdale
Robert Roulston
John Russell
Graeme Sampieri
Mark Sampieri
Adam Sangster
Bernard Saundry
Ian Scroggie
Peter Seers
Todd Shelton
Michael Sholly
Garry Sidwell
Rob Slade
Les Smith
Michael Smith
Brad Spicer
John Stewart
George Sturesteps
John Sutcliffe
Michael Symons
Ross Teitzel
Brock Thompson
Adam Tims
Michael Tong
Geoff Tucker
Larry Tyler
Peter Vogl
Mark Walkley
David Wallace
Michael Walton
Ken Ward
Scott Whiteman
Glenn Whittenbury
Tim Wildash
Max Williams
Craig Willis
Peter Wilson
Doug Wright
Alan Young

SPONSORS

Betta Stone

Honan insurancegroup

L.U.SIMON BUILDERS

Mercedes-Benz Mornington

changingplaces